WELCOME TO THE
CREATIVE CLUB

WELCOME TO THE CREATIVE CLUB

Make Life Your Biggest Art Project

Pia Mailhot-Leichter

MANUSCRIPTS
PRESS

WELCOME TO THE CREATIVE CLUB
Make Life Your Biggest Art Project

ISBN 979-8-88926-228-2 *Paperback*

979-8-88926-229-9 *Hardcover*

979-8-88926-227-5 *Ebook*

For my mother, who ran with wild horses and taught me how to be free.

contents

"I think everything in life is art. What you do. How you dress. The way you love someone, and how you talk. Your smile and your personality. What you believe in, and all your dreams. The way you drink your tea. How you decorate your home. Or party. Your grocery list. The food you make. How your writing looks. And the way you feel. Life is art."

—HELENA BONHAM CARTER

"I want to think again of dangerous and noble things. I want to be light and frolicsome. I want to be improbable, beautiful and afraid of nothing, as though I had wings."

—MARY OLIVER

RSVP

art is
an invitation
to a place where:
we draw shapes
on fogged up windows
learn new languages
whispered in the breeze
write the story of our bones
on screens, in blue light
dance down grocery aisles
shaking a bag of popcorn like a pom-pom
marvel at a cracked pomegranate
and our stained fingertip whorls
hold a pearly seashell to our ears
to hear the ocean's poetry
make cherry clafoutis
in memory of someone we loved.

How we live is our art
the purest form of creation
made in Egyptian cotton sheets
and inside stars before Earth was born.

welcome to the club

Seven years ago, I found my freedom in Siberia. I'm in a third-class rail car because, according to a guidebook, it is where *real* Russia is experienced. Right now, real Russia looks like a man with a yellow pit-stained T-shirt punching the steel car while cradling a bottle of vodka. Thanks to my New York City upbringing, this scene doesn't faze me.

A young Korean woman hurries toward me, hands tightly clasped, and takes a nearby seat. "Are we okay?" she whispers. "Is this man dangerous?"

I soften my gaze. "It's going to be okay. Just avoid eye contact. He'll sleep it off soon enough. You can sit with me if it makes you more comfortable."

I look out the window into the blurred white landscape, avoiding the socks swaying on the rail of a bunk bed and the man clipping his toenails beneath them.

She nods, jaw clenched, and walks back to her bed.

I'm traveling on one of many trains I take across China, Mongolia, and Russia over four weeks. I left the shell of a relationship, dark Copenhagen, and the six-figure creative director and partner job I was fired from behind. I receive severance pay, so technically, I shouldn't be out of the country, which means no selfies. I don't know how my soon-to-be-official ex and I will sell our apartment. But I know this: I had to leave. I was caught in a jail cell I put myself in. This Trans-Siberian rail trip was my handmade *Get Out of Jail Free* card.

It is liberating. I stop scratching the side of my right thumb until it is pink. I fall asleep without Advil PM. I no longer have to pause, breathe deeply, and brace myself before unlocking the door to our apartment.

I don't have to steady myself on the banister every morning as I climb to a workplace I don't feel comfortable or right in.

When I was fired from my job as creative director, fear lost its chokehold on me. I stopped and saw that every aspect of my life, from my relationship to my career, looked like the inside of a toilet bowl after a night drinking tequila from a bottle with a little hat. I was forced to let go of my tight grip on life, and instead of drowning, I float.

Now, I stare at clouds outside a dusty window on a train hurtling through Siberia. This drunk, *vashe zdorov'ye* shouting, knuckle-bleeding Russian man is my beautiful white flag. It's here, in this metal dormitory, among the clink of bottles, smoked fish, and sour perspiration, that I realize *I'm creatively directing my life.* Somewhere, in my bones and the enamel of my teeth, in the most solid parts of me, I know I am going to be okay.

I find God while eating sweet chili Cup of Noodles outside a yurt. One evening, in the Gobi Desert, a retired drama teacher based in Thailand but originally from Australia points to star nurseries in the Orion belt and tells me the word for sky in Mongolian, *tengri*, also means God. Staring at an endless velvet sky pin pricked with starlight, I understand why.

I don't eat mutton, so yet another Cup of Noodles warms my thighs. I dig my shoes into the sand, nod at the camel to my left, and feel the goosebumps of freedom. I created this experience. I brought myself here, and I am not alone in it. Wild dogs yelp as if on cue. Despite the shiver in my spine, I feel stronger and more alive than I've felt in years. Somehow, I forgot how damn powerful and creative I am. This forgetting kept me strapped in the passenger seat of a rusty Buick—not daring to ask "Are we there yet?" Waiting to arrive at that place where life feels safe, fulfilling, and free.

I used to think life was happening *to me*.

I accepted what life threw at me, usually with a gapped-tooth smile. As a nomadic only child cycling through eight different schools, I learned to squeeze into any space. I never knew I had a say in my life's design. After all, I was just a kid. As I grew, I made the best of it but became disconnected, stumbling in the dark for the light switch. I lived on autopilot, informed by inherited stories and beliefs, surviving on chaos and Cheerios and sophisticated childhood programming *because that's what I knew*. I didn't know there was another way.

Until things started to break and the cracks helped me see.

It started when I blew up my marriage to escape, ran for cover into an unhealthy rebound relationship, fell head first into building a creative agency, got lost in the glow of parties and late-night smoke, and luckily stumbled into the office of an amazing therapist. Getting fired was the final break in a series of crashes. It made the growing pile of unhappiness I swept under the rug impossible to ignore. I was thrown through the windshield. Sitting among the shards, I was forced to take a good, hard look at myself and my life. Nothing felt right.

On my four-week solo Trans-Siberian rail ride, I not only found but created myself and my life again. The active, conscious choice to leave and follow a bucket list desire, to take a risk, stick out my tongue, and give fear the middle finger was my first act as the creative director of my life. Not bad, right? I was a passenger on the train, but I was no longer willing to take that seat in life. No more running, no more moving, and no more hiding. No more knee-jerk reactivity, or following someone's script, or activating cruise control. I started applying creativity to design my life.

Creativity is an act, a communion, an awakening. It's a way of being with and in the world. Activating your Creative Club card is your choice.

But if you do it, you reclaim agency, design your experience, and trust something beyond yourself. Whether you call it the universe, the G-O-D, the source, or the OG creator, recognize you are in a process of cocreation. There is no such thing as a lone genius. I might have bought the ticket, but the universe got tired of watching my reruns and shoved me out of a draining job so I could take stock and choose how I wanted to direct the next scene.

Let's have a little heart-to-heart

Hopefully, you won't need dramatic life events, from divorce to being fired, to remind you to *choose* what you want to do with your one precious life—and creatively direct it. Studies show that wisdom is developed by coping with and overcoming adversity. This includes intellectual humility, open-mindedness, understanding the multiple ways in which situations may unfold, and empathy.[1] Now, you don't need adversity to claim your creativity, because it lives within you. But if you have been through some shit, know it's been strengthening your inner Yoda and preparing you to direct what's next.

This book is an urgent nudge to stand in your creative power and design a life dripping with meaning *without deferring happiness* as you create it. Because if you don't, you'll be following someone else's pattern, and there's nothing more soul-crushing than outsourcing your creative agency. We all have a hidden expiration date, so you have one shot at this. This book is whispering—okay, maybe heckling—"Enter stage left."

You won't be creating alone.

I am not an expert, a famous person, or a guru. I am just one woman who went through a beautiful and terrifying full-flavor life hoping to remind you of your innate creativity. I'm right here with you, practicing, stumbling, and relearning while living the juiciest, sweetest version of life I can imagine. It's more Six Flags than a walk in the park. I'm often between two places: arms waving wildly in the air or holding my breath, eyes squeezed shut.

Everything you go through, the bruises and the beauty marks, gives you exactly what you need to serve the world in the way only you can. Creativity is alchemic. It is turning lead into gold, or shit into fertilizer to grow pink peonies. As a recovering creative nomad who needed to reinvent myself over and over again, I have been gifted with the unique ability to combine imagination with action to create new realities. Now, I apply it in my work as a creative midwife for visionary executives, founders, and creatives to bring their brands, businesses, art, and dreams to life. Together, we make *shift* happen. Creativity is the art of transformation, taking "no-thing," an abstract idea, and turning it into "some-thing," whether a product, poem, book, or business plan.

I worked for over a decade in creative agencies. I've built a creative studio, teams, and brands, won numerous awards, and judged award competitions. Somewhere along the line, I hit a ceiling and broke through it to build my own business, Kollektiv Studio. It was time to channel my creativity into building my own dream. After being called to the adventure of coaching, I deepened my art of transformation. I learned inner shifts create outer transformation. Because once you've changed, everything changes, and the *most* creative act is designing your experience of life.

This book is an invitation to make life your biggest art project.

You might have felt the call for change for a while now, that incessant tug on your inner sleeve. Thoughts of what you *could* create visit you at night as soon as your head hits the pillow. You might be on the fence or the cliff's edge in need of a guiding cheerleader. Maybe you've achieved success and are wondering "Is this it?" or you're tired of building someone else's dream and feel ready-not-ready to leap, try, and create.

You might feel lonely, stuck, or deeply aware of what you are capable of, but something is getting in your way. Maybe you downsized your bigness to fit in, play it safe, and not rock the boat, slowly and imperceptibly disconnecting from your creativity, power, and agency as routine and responsibility overshadowed risk and awe. Most importantly, you're ready to do something about it. If any of this sounds like you, welcome. You are in the right place.

I am inviting you to reclaim what has always been yours, fling open the doors of what was once considered an exclusive club, and sit in the plush creative director's chair sipping on a French 75 champagne cocktail, Japanese single malt whiskey, or virgin piña colada, whatever floats your boat. You get to choose.

As you move through the book, you'll experience subtle shifts until suddenly, everything's changed. My life experiences and lessons lead the way, and poetic pit stops give you a different view of the creative process. This anti-how-to guide is packed with neuroscience research, creative coaching talks, and applicable fieldwork. At the end of our journey together, your life will become your biggest art project yet.

You already have everything you need, which is good, because *only you* can create this art project. I don't have the answers. You do. I'm simply guiding you to them.

So, let's do it.

Take a deep breath, trust yourself, and buckle up.

Your journey to living creatively starts here.

you're a card-carrying member

I discover my creativity while fully dressed in a pool.

I'm eight years old, sitting in a sleek hotel bar on the beach in San Juan, feet swinging in the air, wondering why anyone would want to swim in a pool when the ocean is a few feet away. The splash surprises everyone at the bar. One moment, my mother is on a bar stool, a glass of white wine sweating in hand; the next she is in the pool, fully dressed. My mother bobs, white T-shirt glued to round breasts, blonde hair plastered and slick, a lazy smile on her face. Everyone stares. My cheeks burn and heart races. I have no idea what to do.

My mother waves and spits chlorinated water. "Come in!" she shouts. "It's so refreshing!"

I walk over to the kidney-shaped pool and bend down to whisper into her ear. "Mom, don't you think we should go home now?"

"Don't be such a party pooper. It's just a little swim. Plus, it's hot."

"But we could take a walk on the beach and swim in the ocean instead." I kneel closer to the pool's edge to grab her hand and help her out. "Wouldn't that be nice? Please?"

She reaches her dripping hand upward and wraps her fingers around my arm. I think that, for one shining moment, my mom is going to listen to me. Just as I yank her arm upward, she pulls me down into the water, glitter jelly shoes and all.

The water shocks me. My senses are stunned as I resurface, suck in air, and struggle to doggie paddle. Mom holds on tight. "Let go! It's not funny." I try to break free. My shoes are heavy and clothes sticky, and random stares burn into the back of my head.

"Everyone is staring!"

"Who cares? We're allowed to swim. It's fun."

She won't let go, and none of the bystanders will put down their martini glasses to help. I'm on my own in the deep end.

Then the idea strikes.

I stop resisting. "Do you want to play a game?" She pauses, intrigued. "We'll race to the end of the pool. It'll be fun. Okay?" Then the real twist: "I bet I'll win."

My competitive mother loosens her grip. "That's what you think," she says with a smirk. "On the count of one… two… three!"

We're off. I reach the other end of the pool in no time flat. Now beyond her reach, I pull myself out of the water. I leave my mom behind and walk on the beach toward home. A few minutes later, my mother zigzags in the sand beside me.

"You're no fun," she says and runs ahead, leaving me to walk home alone. I seek sympathy from the seagulls obliviously picking at a Snickers wrapper, my heart heavier than my wet clothes. The sun beats on my skin and tears burn, yet I am relieved. A moment that lasted less than ten minutes but felt like forever is now done. My body slackens. I'm flooded with a weird sense of pride.

That little girl swimming with her shoes on learned that **creativity is not just something we do; it is how we respond to the challenges in life.**

Creativity is what makes us human.

"Every human being has a deep-seated biological urge to develop novel, useful, and sometimes beautiful solutions to everyday challenges."[1]

Scientists have discovered the "creativity genes" that make us uniquely human, distinguishing us from chimpanzees and Neanderthals. These genes activate self-awareness processes that allow *Homo sapiens* to "be creative in narrative art and science." The researchers determined these genes were selected because of advantages tied to greater creativity, prosocial behavior, and healthy longevity.[2]

We're hardwired for creativity. All of us are.

If you're human, you're a creative artist at work. Whether you've allowed that innate part of you to come out and play is on you. If you haven't, I get it. It's not surprising given the creative myths that prevail in our culture. We not only put creatives in a box, but we also pack creativity into one, snapping bubble wrap as we place the prize inside cardboard walls. We often confine creativity to the realm of velvet beret-wearing artists, but creativity colors every aspect of our lives. "Creativity is sometimes seen as synonymous with arts, ignoring the fact that creativity can be expressed in virtually any domain, such as in science, social relationships, or even crime."[3]

Now, with modern neuroscience, creativity can be assessed and measured to debunk myths that keep your creativity under wraps. Neuroscience studies have identified specific brain networks involved in the creative process, most notably the default mode network (DMN).[4] The fact this network is present in all humans indicates a biological basis for creativity. Our ability to imagine, daydream, and think divergently is not confined to a gifted few but is a fundamental aspect of the human mind.

The media's portrayal of geniuses and prodigies fuels the popular belief that creativity is selectively handed out. One study found that the more stories people read about this kind of exceptional big-C "Creativity," the more they believe creativity to be a fixed trait. "A mounting body of research shows that creativity is not a fixed character trait, nor is it a reserve that we deplete as we grow older."[5] It's a learned skill we can develop and nurture over time. And I'd take it even further. Creativity isn't just something we cultivate; it's who we are.

Creativity is not just something you do; it's a way of being. It's how you respond to the challenges and circumstances of life. You're in constant creative response with your experience. Sometimes, it might seem like you're out of control, like a hand-wrenching eight-year-old girl fully dressed in a pool, but also like her, you get to creatively respond to the circumstances you find yourself in. As adults, we can shape our realities as well as creatively respond to challenges we're presented with. When we recognize our ability to craft our artful response *and* creatively direct our experience, we start writing our own script.

Let's talk (get all creative coach-y with it)

So, why even care about what's creative or what isn't?

Because believing you're *not* creative is what limits you. Often, that belief stems from fear of judgment or failure.

Believing you *are* creative is the most critical step in designing your life. If you don't claim your innate creative talent, you won't use it. It can be easier to believe the creativity gene skipped you, because then you don't have to create what you *really* want to make and risk failure or ridicule. You can simply say, "I'm not creative."

If you deny your creative power, you can't wield it. This is a gate you need to walk through to reconnect with your creativity and start building your dream. When you connect to your innate creativity, you're empowered to design your life, your days, and your one experience of this life. *And that's what I am inviting you to do.*

The first step is to recognize you're a card-carrying member of the Creative Club. Welcome. The second is to flash it often.

You are a natural-born creative. The way you plan weekly meals, dance in the kitchen, choose what to wear, swagger into a room; how your hands move when you speak, sing in the bathroom, drive on the freeway—all your creation, your unique signature.

How you live your life is your biggest contribution to the gallery of existence. It creates an impact, a ripple effect, known and unknown. It's in the way you smile at a stranger, handle your name being misspelled on a coffee cup, hold your partner, and walk down the aisle of a grocery store. You create every day, whether it's composing an email (not a symphony but a composition nonetheless), cooking, or planning your schedule.

Creativity is *not* something outside of you. Connecting to the sweet essence (or cedar wood and leather) of who you are—beyond titles, roles, citizenship, denomination, alma mater, and gender—taps into your raw creativity.

When you return home to yourself and reconnect to what really matters, your creativity is unleashed. What makes your life, art, or business unique is your own flavor, your own brand of delightful weirdness. You hold the recipe to the secret sauce.

Your job is to get closer to the magic that is you:
what you really want
what you need
what holds you back
what sets you on fire
what snuffs you out
what motivates you
what repels you
what riles you up
what you stand for
what you dream of
what world you want to create
what you want to leave behind
what makes your heart beat faster
what makes you squirm
what contracts and expands you
what calls out to you

From that resonant, redolent place, your creativity rises to meet you. It comes forth, pours out, and infuses your life with your musky aroma. The process feels right, even if you don't know where it will take you, and you're ready for the joy ride.

Creativity is how you respond to life:
what you do with your pain
how you choose to be in the present moment
which balls you catch or let fall
how you show up every day
how you perceive the world
the stories you tell and live
solving everyday problems in new ways
All creative, all you.

Your life is the ultimate canvas.

There is nothing more radical, revolutionary, or creative than designing your life. You are always creating, from the moment you wake up to when your head hits the pillow and your subconscious brushstrokes your dreams. You're just not *consciously* creating—yet. But when you start, when you realize and actualize your agency and innate ability as a *creator*, shit really starts to get real, and your life changes form.

There are tools and practices, concepts, and insights that support you in claiming, nurturing, and applying your innate creativity so you can make life your grand masterpiece. There are also ideas, beliefs, and cultural stories that keep you from tapping into your creative power. We're going to look at it all, so by the end of this book, you're no longer reading from someone else's script but writing your own.

Fieldwork

Keep a journal for a week. Write down any new or random ideas that pop into your head. At the end of each day, review your ideas and filter through them. After the week is up, pick a few of your favorite ones. This could be a new recipe, an essay, a business idea anything at all. When you find an idea that really excites you, map out the steps toward making it real and then do the most needle-moving action daily.

Carve out creative space and time. Design a space at home dedicated exclusively to your creative work. Visit it daily, whether for ten minutes or two hours. Decorate it in ways that inspire and motivate you. Hopefully, it has a door you can close to the world when you need to go into your creative cave.

Write a script that feeds your creativity. Pinpoint the beliefs or ideas that stop you from being creative and write the inverse. For example, if the belief is "I'm not creative," flip it to "I'm naturally creative," or turn "It's hard for me to come up with ideas" into 'Ideas flow easily to me." Read from it daily. Observe the impact.

come on in, the water's warm
A poem for those on the ledge

Left foot dangling in the air,
wind styling hair,
the heart, a piñata,
littering crepe paper and candy
over terracotta dirt.

Right leg muscles tense
stubbornly fixed to the ground
fear increases heart beats
uncertainty
makes jeans stick to skin,
heavy.

Standing between here and there
is a strange limbo,
a violent tug on both ends of a rope
one side wants to stay put,
the other craves the wind.

Until the struggle between limbs
hurts more than the leap itself—
so you say "Fuck it!"
and launch, knees tucked,
cannonballing into the sea.

You float, buoyed by a current
stare at animal-shaped clouds,
follow the choreography of seagulls.

Once you're in, you won't want
to return to dry land.
Even when you're sputtering salt water,
sunburnt and peeling,
nothing beats the view of the sky,
the rhythm of foam-crested waves,
and a pastel horizon of possibility.

You don't know what's next
and that's precisely why
you feel most alive
in the ocean of your choosing,
surfing on the curl of your creativity.

If you're ready to dive
into your own big wide,
I'm the one in the donut floatie
smelling like piña coladas
windswept and freckled,
waving wildly.

blackjack and the MoMA

My dad said he didn't choose art; art chose him. I hoped I wouldn't be picked. It's 1981, I'm six years old, and I love doodling on the Metropolitan Museum of Art (MET) pad, where my dad works as a security guard to give him time to paint. He'd sneak me into the closed wings of the MET, leading me into magical worlds of colors and shapes. It's better than his last gig working for the mob as a blackjack dealer, sometimes with one foot out the door when a corrupt cop informed them of a police raid.

We're in my dad's loft on the Bowery. A huge fake palm tree leaf hangs from the ceiling above a striped Peruvian wool hammock, and paintings line brick walls. Dad stands before a canvas, jeans covered in paint, Stevie Wonder playing in the background. Wonder's *Song of Life* album is also where my dad keeps his secret stash of money in case we're robbed. He's intensely focused on the canvas in front of him.

The world feels safe when he paints. He is enraptured, lost in time, hands fluttering bird-like above the canvas. When my dad's brush strokes, he is in a world of his own making, riding high above the siren sounds drifting in through the windows. In this clearing, I write or play, the smell of coffee and crayons in the air. At some point, usually when he completes his latest piece, he'll crash land into depression until he rises again, pulled by the paintbrush in his hand.

After selling a piece or landing a show, he'd get a rush of energy, a manic joy that leads him to chase me around the long butcher's table in the kitchen and laugh as I squeal. He'd make his signature chicken parmigiana using fresh ingredients from shops in Little Italy, always heaping too much food on my plate, with classical music playing on the radio. He told jokes and sang the blues, spilling wine on the red and white checkered tablecloth, shaking the vase of fresh flowers.

For a moment, I take the place of his art, his full attention focused on me. Joy spread across his face as he watched me struggle with strings of melted mozzarella. When we eat together, he lets the phone go to the machine if it rings. Our time together is paramount.

I try to ride his waves. I attempt to lift him up with a song when he's down and harmonize my giggles and enthusiasm with his glee when the tide is up. Often, I have nightmares, usually of being chased, a faceless perp steadily gaining on me as I tire from running through trees. Just as he's about to catch me, I wake up in a sweat. Sometimes, I sneak into my dad's bed and try to remain as still as possible. Otherwise, I'll get sent back to my room and my imagination, where the wild things live.

When he refuses to sell his work to someone he doesn't like, or has to find another way to make ends meet working as a horse and carriage driver in Central Park for one, his rage sizzles and wires blow. He once walked over the hood of a car when it stopped in a pedestrian crossing to make a point, my cheeks flushing as I froze in place. Watching him make a living from art feels like being on the Cyclone, the second-steepest wooden roller coaster in the world at Coney Island.[1] I can almost hear the click-click-clicking sound as he climbs upward and the screech of his descent.

His impulse to paint goes beyond the desire to be famous and seen, although every artist wants the world to experience their work. Unbeknownst to him, he reached the height of his career in 1972, three years before my arrival, when his art was exhibited in the Christmas Show at the Museum of Modern Art (MoMA).[2] Despite a grant from the Pollock-Krasner Foundation in 1999, he never soared as high as he did in his early career. I've seen his heart break when canvases are relegated to storage and burst in one-man shows. He's both my hero and warning signal.

I'm often asked if my dad's creativity was passed down to me, as if it was genetic. As a kid, this annoyed me, as though I was meant to replicate the genius and mania of my father's mode of expression. As if it was expected of me as *his* daughter. I was not my own but fated to follow his path. Without understanding the concept of predestination, I knew what it felt like: not getting to choose for myself. I wasn't about to reject creativity. I loved doodling, writing poems inspired by Shel Silverstein, and illustrating castles for my stories about faraway lands where the princess didn't need a kiss to wake up, but I didn't want to accept the pain that came with it.

So, I'd grumble, "*No*, I write."

What I didn't realize is that my dad's art didn't fuel his depression and anxiety. It kept it at bay. And my father is a gifted artist but not a stellar businessman. As a kid, witnessing what he sacrificed tells me another story, one that is pervaded by culture: the myth of the tortured artist.

Creativity is not only viewed as a rare, divine gift reserved for a few geniuses but is often linked to madness. The long-standing myth that creativity is linked to suffering is perpetuated by stories of famous artists who struggled with mental health issues.[3]

Think of Sylvia Plath, Kurt Cobain, and Vincent van Gogh. The autistic Mozart, the depressed Beethoven, the tortured Poe. Like Kafka, Michelangelo, Woolf, and Hemingway, they all faced anguish, torment, addiction, mania, and madness at some point in their lives. Throw in a quote from Aristotle, "'No great mind has ever existed without a touch of madness,' and we have the making of a mythconception."[4]

Research shows that creativity is linked more to well-being than to being a tortured soul. Studies reveal that while mental illness can sometimes coincide with great art, creativity is generally tied to "positive emotions and well-being... Researchers have found that people reported feeling happy and energized during everyday creative endeavors, and that being in a positive mood goes hand in hand with creative thinking."[5]

A study showed that people engaged in creative activities had increased positive emotion the next day, "suggesting that everyday creativity leads to well-being rather than the other way around." It also discovered that creativity boosts well-being for everyone regardless of personality type. "This suggests that everyone and anyone can benefit from introducing creativity into their daily lives."[6]

The idea that artists have to suffer to create is a myth that ignores the hard work and agency of creative people like us. People often see creativity as a spontaneous, fixed trait, but research shows it's a skill you can develop and nurture over time, no matter how you're feeling.[7] Many people think they need to be in a specific mood to produce anything worthwhile. The problem is, we can't always control our feelings, but we can control our actions. Sometimes, our actions can even change how we feel. The truth is that living a creative life isn't just about thinking; it's about doing. As marketing guru Seth Godin puts it, "Creativity is an action, not a feeling."[8]

My dad understands this. Taking action to create art saves my father from the abyss of his depression. Painting pulls him up and back into the world. When he stops painting, he falls into a darkness I am afraid he won't get out of. Making art turns his light back on. His prolific creativity is not fueled by suffering or illness. It's what shows him the way out of it.

Creativity is a choice.

A choice I was scared to make. My dad followed his passion, but it cost him financial security. I believed that was the price of following a dream that colored beyond the lines of society's prescriptive book. Follow the status quo or pay the hefty rebellion tax. So, I went the other route, commercial creativity, hoping to have both creativity and a steady paycheck. And it did pay, for a while.

It's the summer of 2019, and our agency is at the Cannes Lions International Festival of Creativity, the biggest and most prestigious advertising award show, or as they describe it, "the destination for anyone in the pursuit of creative excellence."[9] The agency's creatives, including myself, have been flown to Cannes for the festivities. As we're walking along the pier, swaying like the palm trees above us, Richard—a Swedish brand designer wearing Doc Martens, a tight-fitting white tank top, and a gold chain—screams *"Livet!"* which means "to live" in Swedish. He raises a bottle of rosé and pours it out, making it rain pink.

He turns to us, smiling hazily through his ginger handlebar mustache, and we erupt in a fit of side-aching laughter. We crash a yacht party, the DJ spins house beats, white lights along the masts compete with the flash of sequined dresses. We're about to step onto the golden deck, but the host insists we remove our shoes so as not to damage the floorboards. Richard refuses to take off his Docs, and we are forcibly removed. On to the next one.

It's intoxicating. I get high on the supply and lose myself in ten-hour days and weekend pitch work. The parties, the lifestyle—it feels like being part of a family, which is a smart corporate move because I pour everything I have into it. For a while, it gives me what I longed for as a nomadic only child: a place to belong where I can create, be safe, be a cool kid, and earn a good living. Although, just like being half Jewish, I never feel creative enough.

Winning feels good. The golden sheen of awards warms the vampiric skin I acquired after long nights wrangling pitches. Even though I never took home a Lion at Cannes, I feel the rush of standing on stage, being recognized by peers, and being invited to judge other award shows. I'd rub shoulders with revered commercial creatives who said they'd rather be at the Cannes *Film* Festival but settled for the next best—and safer—thing.

My creativity was confined to client briefs.

Given the long hours at the agency and after-work drinks, I never managed to write my own work in the evenings, so I settled into what felt like good enough at the time. I was too busy acting in the world to stop, sit, and commit to my creativity outside of work.

Settling is the easier choice, because when it comes to creating and relying on your craft, there's a lot at risk: the ego, survival, and potential disappointment in not being able to make it. Not trying is the safer bet, and imagining what might have happened if you did is a sweet fantasy world you can inhabit when you're not at the agency.

I tell myself that my unfinished poems could have been as successful as Rupi Kaur's book. I imagine being on stage looking out at the audience, all on the edge of their seats, waiting with bated breath to take the mic. I extract some thirst-quenching juice from the idea of what might have been, so I don't have to take a chance, bet on myself, and actually see what would happen if I put myself out there and try. So, I stay put at the Gutter Bar at Cannes, nodding at the cute TV ad music producer from Berlin as he describes his process and longingly stares into his empty glass.

I'm born creative just like you, but I let go of the dream of becoming a writer, instead choosing the safer, well-paved road. My dad showed me that doing what you love costs, but it doesn't have to. I never aspired to become an independent creative living from my craft, because I never allowed myself such aspirations. I didn't realize it was a festering dream. The entry fee for the dream arena is doing things you have never done before and having no idea how it will turn out. I am redefining what creativity means to me. It doesn't have to be a sacrifice, nor does it require suffering. It can be whatever you want it to be; whatever you need it to be.

everything is available
at the 7-Eleven within

Imagine you're inside the 7-Eleven of your mind. Slurpee machines whirring, the smell of burnt hazelnut coffee and sweaty hot dogs heavy in the air. Your feet stick to spilled Big Gulps as you approach the counter. The clerk, rubbing a dime on a scratch-off game, looks up and says, "I've heard you've been thinking about creating something. Nagging, repeating thoughts. Becoming almost impossible to drown out." He shakes his head. "Just like the damn door ringing every time it opens. So why don't you just do it already?"

You stare at the glistening rows of cigarettes behind him and say, "Every idea has already been created, so why bother? I'd just be adding cilantro to last night's chili sin carne. Where will I find the idea for that business, book, or new track? See? I don't even know what it is!"

The clerk chucks the game in the garbage. "Damn, I was so close!" He opens his arms wide and says, "Come on, now. Look around you. Everything you need is right here. Endless possibilities. How did you think we came up with Big Bites? We branded regular old hot dogs, *et voilà*, a bestseller."

"Fine, okay, it's possible. But if I do, when will I actually have time to create it? Have you seen my schedule? I have a real job, and I am angling for that bonus. Just a few more months, then maybe I'll have time for it."

The clerk leans forward, freckled elbows on the counter, gets real close, and whispers, "Bullshit."

Blood rushes to your face, spit flying as you say, "In the real adulting world, you gotta make sacrifices. This is not some low-stakes grocery store peddling sugar and gas, where we get to play lottery games, drink absurdly-sized cola, and listen to door chimes. This is reality."

Billy, or so says the white plastic name tag pinned on his red polo, laughs and says, "That ain't even your story. The least creative act ever is parroting." His finger wags, and in a nasal voice, he says, "The world is a tough place. Money doesn't grow on trees. You gotta work hard to make ends meet. Following your passion is for trust-fund kids and bums. Yada, yada, yada."

"So what am I supposed to do? Just make up my own stories?"

Billy pulls the toothpick out of his mouth, points it at you, and says, "Bingo."

I've experienced this inner dialogue too. We all have a Billy or inner wise one (whatever form it might take) who can guide us back to our knowing, challenge our bullshit, and help us recognize the stories we're telling ourselves. This conversation can shape the fabric of your reality because what you *believe* to be true about yourself and the world creates your *experience* of it.

As a kid with an artist father and a mother who was one of ten children from a small Québec countryside town, money in my family was scarce. It was something to be saved and put aside, just in case. When my parents and I went out for dinner, I'd order the cheapest thing on the menu. My mother checked grocery bills, sometimes swapped price tags on items in stores, and bought clothing from secondhand stores or *only* when on sale. My father didn't have a credit card for most of his life because he didn't trust financial institutions.

These ideas stayed with me. I never questioned their veracity. I inherited the behaviors and perpetuated the belief that there wasn't enough, which made me feel anxious and fearful about money. I always put money aside and felt relieved when numbers increased in a spreadsheet.

Every time I played the game of guessing how much the groceries would cost at the register; every time I wouldn't allow myself to order what I really wanted (what can I say? I have expensive taste); every time I refused to buy things unless they were on sale, I was sending out messages—*I'm not worth it. There's not enough. I don't trust life has my back.* This reinforced the belief, deepening that mental groove again and again.

Even though I received six months' severance pay after being fired from my partner and creative director role, grossing $11 thousand a month, I didn't take a first-class train on the Trans-Siberian or stay in the Four Seasons in Moscow (though I did see ballet at the Bolshoi Theater) but stayed in hostels, one-star hotels, and home stays across China, Mongolia, and Russia. Although they all led to amazing adventures, some I recounted here, I didn't allow myself to experience luxury, comfort, or a different kind of pleasure because I didn't have a job waiting for me, so I gripped what felt like safety to me—money—at the expense of my experience.

Looking back on my Trans-Siberian trip, I could have easily splurged. But if I did, it wouldn't have felt good, causing me more stress and anxiety. How crazy is that?

"You can imagine it's not a very pleasant place to be, to be kind of on guard, thinking that you've got to keep everything you have, that you're going to lose it in some way," says Susan Greenhalgh, an accredited financial counselor and founder of Mind Your Money LLC in Providence, Rhode Island. "That's kind of a vigilant standpoint, and that's a very difficult standpoint to enjoy life from."[1]

I was imprisoned by my own beliefs and fears. I needed to learn how to create safety within and start trusting myself and life after years of bracing for impact.

So, how did I rewrite that script? Coaching certification made me brutally aware of the scarcity script I was playing out. I took the first coaching course, reassured by its money-back guarantee. When I had to make the decision to invest $10 thousand after already investing $5 thousand, I felt stuck, scared, and unsure of what to do. I asked a friend and coach, Martina, who had been through certification, for help. We met by the lakes in Copenhagen, walking along the water, past spandex suctioned runners and mamas in cashmere sweaters with babies in expensive strollers.

"Martina, I don't know if I can invest this much."

Her hazel eyes met mine. "What's stopping you?"

I gazed at the dirty swan on a pile of floating bottles. "What if it doesn't work out? What if I don't make the money back? What if I can't use it?"

"What does your gut say?"

"It says go for it. This lights you up."

"So, that's clear. Then what's really going on here? No matter what, this is an investment in yourself. Are you questioning if you're worth it?"

I sighed. "I guess so."

I see my money wound clearly for the first time. The decision to invest in myself, in the program, was the first big step toward rewriting the belief. If I believe money is abundant, an energy that flows when unblocked; if I trust the universe has my back; and most importantly, if I believe in myself, why *wouldn't* I do this? Fear, that's why. When I see fear, disrobed, standing naked, no disguises, no wardrobe changes, goose-pimpled and exposed, I take one look at its shriveled dick and say, "Hell no, you're not running me anymore." And so begins the work of trusting enough to let go.

The scarcity script isn't unique to my parents and me. It's a pervasive cultural story that fuels our economy. Modern economics hinges on the scarcity principle: humans have endless desires but limited resources. Economists often argue that more economic growth is the long-term solution to global poverty. This focus on economic expansion paints our history as a relentless pursuit of more, but anthropological evidence tells a different story.

Through the chemical analysis of bones, social scientists have "demonstrated conclusively that early humans were not constantly teetering on the brink of starvation."[2] On the contrary, they ate well despite having only a few stone and wooden implements at their disposal. Our ancestors, instead of merely surviving in a scarce and dangerous world, were living the good life.

In his book *Work: A Deep History, from the Stone Age to the Age of Robots,* anthropologist James Suzman reveals that for much of human history, we lived as hunter-gatherers, unconcerned with economic growth. Instead of working long hours to accumulate more, our natural inclination has been to do the minimum amount of work necessary to underwrite a good life. When people had an abundance of goods, they often saw them not as resources for economic growth, "but rather as so many excuses to throw gigantic parties, like the ones that presumably took place at... Stonehenge. In many cultures, giving away or even ritualistically destroying one's possessions at festivals has been a common way to show one's worth."[3]

Our ancestors show us we're not wired for scarcity. How we'll arrive at a post-scarcity society, and if we'll manage to shift course before we "[eat] our way right through the biosphere," as Aaron Benanav, researcher at Humboldt University of Berlin and author of *Automation and the Future of Work*, puts it, is yet to be seen.[4] But we can start by shifting our own story and relationship with resources, money, and life. When we are freed from the idea that time and money are inherently scarce, we take more creative risks and, like our hunter-gatherer ancestors, optimize for a good life.

It starts with changing your relationship with money.

Financial coach Linda Garcia healed her emotional relationship with money, transforming it from a painful source of lack into fuel for growth and dreams.

Growing up, Garcia watched her parents stretch every dollar to keep the family afloat. This upbringing led her to believe there would never be enough money, creating stress and anxiety about finances. As a former marketing executive in TV and film, Garcia earned a good living and had funds for passion projects. Yet, her scarcity mindset held her back from pursuing her dreams and living her purpose. [5]

Starting her own business changed everything. Garcia realized she needed to spend money to help her company grow. "We think that we have to work to obtain money, but wealthy people know that the opposite is true: You have to let go of money, invest it, in order to duplicate it. But that starts with letting go of the scarcity mindset and one's emotional relationship with money," she says.[6]

My husband, Teddy, is my person and my money healer. I used to tease him, saying that he was born to be rich. He spends money flagrantly, easily, with no hang ups or trip ups. He belongs to a champagne club, receives a new bottle of bubbly every month, fences like a prince in an expensive training center, leases a Mercedes, and allows himself to freely enjoy the finer things in life even though his savings are sparse. He is like a Yip-Yip Martian from *Sesame Street* to me, and I love it. He shows me there is a different way to be with money and life.

I asked Teddy how he developed this trusting relationship with money. He sits, pensive for a moment, thick white blond eyebrows framing serious blue eyes, runs his hand through his long hair, and says, "The worst thing that could happen is if I die tomorrow and there's money in my bank account, because then I haven't spent it." He reaches out for my hand and continues. "That doesn't mean be reckless, but it does mean get that one amazing bottle of champagne and the unforgettable experience it gives you instead of six bottles of shitty Asti and bad hangovers."

I love how Teddy leads me to the buffet of life, encourages me to take the lobster tail, knocking the Tupperware box out of my hand. I'm curious about how he does that when he might not be able to cover the check. "So, how do you spend money confidently when you don't have it?"

He crosses one chino leg over the other, his scent of vanilla tobacco in the air, and says, "I spend money because I trust it will come back. I always trust it will work out somehow." Teddy sees my awestruck expression, winks, and laughs. I go to jab him, but he catches my arm and draws me into him.

I rubbed off on him, so now he checks grocery receipts to make sure we weren't charged for items we didn't buy (it happens more often than you think!). But, hey, old habits die hard. I am learning, easing into trusting, investing in myself and my creativity, and allowing myself to experience luxury and pleasure *freely,* and his influence plays a big role in that. During COVID-19, instead of hoarding toilet paper, Teddy surprised me with take-away dinner from the five-star Hotel

D'Angleterre in Copenhagen, caviar on blini-style. He encourages me to take risks I believe in and enjoy lavish pleasures, like lunch at a Michelin star restaurant on the Aeolian Island of Salina off the coast of Northern Sicily. He reminds me that I am worth it.

Why does this matter? If you're stuck feeling powerless in a fear and scarcity state, whether it comes to money, creativity, or time, how can you assume the creative agency required to design your life experience? It is being designed for you by default.

Scarcity, lack, worth, and general "not enoughness" combine into a pervasive and corrosive belief. Usually, the belief is that you are not enough or worth enough as you are right now. If only you could be your *best* self, get that promotion, land that gig, find that partner, make more money, fill in the blank, then you'll be safe, happy, and good enough. What fills the blank changes frequently. When the thing is attained, a new one takes its place. Because it is not about the goal, it's how achieving it will make you feel. This isn't to say: Don't have goals. I'm saying divorce your worth from the goals. You are worthy as you are, right here, right now.

A generalized fear is that if we stop ferociously pursuing the goal, we'll get lazy and apathetic. But when the starting point is enoughness, and the goal is not to fill a gap or prove your worth, I'd wager the experience of working toward it becomes lighter and more joyful, and the likelihood of success will increase ten-fold. Lack or abundance as a driver can achieve outward success, but the difference is how you feel when you reach said goal.

You don't need to believe you are enough; there is enough, or it is enough to be externally successful. Plenty of people have success but still feel ravenous. It will never feel like enough if lack is your starting point. Acknowledging your "enoughness" is not only a step toward healing within, it is a balm we rub on Earth. The more we mindlessly consume, the less we consciously create.

> *"One of the deepest habitual patterns that we have is to feel that now is not enough."*[7]
>
> —Pema Chödrön

While this book invites you to make life your biggest art project, we're creating together. Imagine the impact of the collective shift from following an outdated and harmful script to writing your own finger-licking fulfilling one on the world? Imagine what happens when you free yourself to create a life that makes your hair stand on end and cheeks ache? When I ask my clients what feels fun or brings them joy, *all* of them list experiences that have almost nothing to do with money besides the occasional long-distance trip. Just realizing this creates a seismic shift.

Let's dig in

Knowing there is enough right now is essential to living a creative life. Creativity itself is an abundant resource. It's not only a part of who you are or how your brain inherently functions but also an energy you can tap into. It's not something to get or be given to you. You already have it. You just have to be brave enough to use it.

My father's art has always been, and still is, abundant. It overflows like a distracted diner waitress pouring coffee. I started writing as a kid and continued throughout my life, even when "just" in the form of journaling. This practice strengthened my belief in the endless creative well within. It was no wonder by the time I landed in my first brainstorm in the advertising world, ideas came gushing out. It starts by believing you have the creative juice within and then letting it flow.

The "not enough" story keeps us doing, chasing, and feeling dissatisfied. It keeps us disconnected, following someone else's pace and narrative. There is not enough time, money, or ideas to go around, and it leaves us hungrily chasing our tails imagining they are hot dogs, never satiated or satisfied because we are looking outside of ourselves.

Scarcity is fear wearing a velvet face mask. When you strip it down, it's a feeling of not enough: I'm not enough, there's not enough, it's not enough. An illusion of being separate and alone. It's having a bad case of the "what-ifs."

- What if I don't make it?
- What if I fail?
- What if I have to go back to a nine-to-five?
- What if I lose everything?
- What if I end up broke and alone?

How do you recognize when you are in the fear or the trust zone? Trust feels like being pulled toward something. Fear feels like being up against it. Creating from fear feels like a hustle, a grind; forcing, pushing, and battling against. Moving with trust feels open, expansive, exciting; like being in flow, in sync, relaxed, and like someone has your back. Fear rushes; trust moves slowly.

Trust is knowing:
- you have everything you need.
- life is abundant.
- it's all here right now.
- all ideas are within you.
- you're not alone in it.
- you're worth it.

There's nowhere to go, nothing to do. Only a way to be. It's having a *good* case of the "what-ifs."

- What if life is conspiring in my favor?
- What if I am right where I am supposed to be?
- What if the universe is working with me, not against me?
- What if everything I need is here and on its way?
- What if I succeed?
- What happens if I *don't* try?

Still not sure of how to notice the difference? Your body delivers energetic cues. Fear feels tight, restrictive, like a gripping; a state of prolonged contraction, breath short and shallow. Trust feels like an exhalation, a release, a surrender; straight back, open shoulders, relaxed muscles, breath slow and deep. Every *body* has its own cues, its own knowing. Explore yours. When fear is present, I feel behind, not where I am supposed to be or "should" be. I start to rush, filling every crevice of my day with a task. Even meditation becomes a to-do.

So how to make the shift? Notice without judgment. "Oh, I'm here." Slow down, take a walk, breathe deeply, and get wildly curious about yourself. Observe and see what happens when you start looking at what's here now. I repeat affirmations. I celebrate myself in some small way. I remember to have fun, dance, and laugh. I might brainstorm thirty things that bring me joy and do one of them immediately. The shift is almost instantaneous. The hardest part is catching myself when I'm in a fear state and stopping to reflect and shift that energy.

If we don't know how it will turn out anyway, we might as well have fun with it. That comes with trust—trusting yourself and life. Otherwise, what's the point? If fun is not enough of a motivator for you, I'll leave you with this: If you don't believe there is enough, you won't have enough to give to others. Isn't life meant to be shared? Why not throw a gigantic Stonehenge party? There is enough love and presence to give and share—*always*.

Fieldwork

Feeling the sting of scarcity? Face your fear and finances (fear shrinks as you walk toward it). Read through recent bank and credit card statements to get a better sense of where your money goes each month and where you might be able to cut or *increase* spending. Do your spending habits align with what you value most?

What belief do you hold about money? Is it helpful or harmful? If the latter, what belief would you *rather* hold? Rescript it. Take one action, big or small, that shows you actually believe it. Repeat frequently and with a healthy dose of common sense.

What if you took money out of the equation? Imagine your bank account is flush. What would you create *now*?

towels are not thrown, but worn around necks
A poem for those entering the arena

She knocks her Jordans against the ring
dust sparkles in the air
revealing purple and yellow leopard print
before stepping into the squared circle.

It's eerily quiet
all peanut shells and empty Gatorade bottles
vacant seats and white towels,
the faint smell of pine
a rusted chair lonely in the corner.

Soon, the spotlights will blind her.
She'll stand in fluorescent lycra
Aqua Net keeping her together
face smeared with Vaseline
gold hoops catching the light
and winking at the crowd.

She leans against the ropes
heavy with hope,
picks at the skin of her thumb.
Sweat trickles down her spine
her temple vein beats to her drum
unsure, uncertain about what's
                              coming next.

guided by the gut

I insisted on wearing a tiara for my first day at elementary school.
My mother sighed and said, "Go on then." I waltzed the halls of P.S. 321
in a long ruffled dress, thick brown hair reaching the small of my back,
head crowned with stones. My mother later told me other moms looked
at her disapprovingly, as if she chose to dress her daughter as a royal
on her inaugural school day. Mom had wanted to say, "My daughter
chose to wear that. I just went with it."

That same year, I told my mom about a bully at school, and with a
wave of her hand, she suggested I speak to the principal and sort it out
myself. After Mr. W's class let out, I waited for my mom after school—
she was late *again*—and that boy in eighth grade taunted me and my
friend Caroline. He picked up a metal rod from the Brooklyn sidewalk,
raised it in the air, and threatened us with it. I stepped up, hands on
hips, all red and white polka-dot dress and lopsided braids, and said,
"Go ahead, hit me. I dare you. If you do, I'll tell the principal, and you'll
be in big trouble." The boy dropped the rod with a clank and ran away.

My mother wasn't actually late that day. She was observing me from
the sidelines, wondering what I'd do. She later told me this was one
of her proudest moments because she knew from then on I'd be okay.
She'd tell that story repeatedly as I grew up, even imitating my lisp.
"Tell the printhipal." My mother always encouraged me to find my own
way but never indicated *how* to find the way. She valued strength and
independence but never showed me how to connect with the compass
within. Especially as a little person, I found it difficult to know what
was "right."

As a kid, I wanted more than anything to be *normal*. I wished my name
was Jennifer, not Pia, and that we lived in a house that smelled like

real chocolate brownies. My mom was drawn to things that challenged what she saw as mediocrity and the norm. She baked pot brownies for her friends, listening to Jacques Brel, red toenails dancing across the floor, singing along with the ash of her cigarette threatening to fall, smoke and Chanel N°5 moving along with her. She cursed Reagan and lamented the end of the hippie era—"We really thought we'd change the world"—when a dream of how life might be lived faded like the dye in T-shirts. She kept her private rebellion alive by partying and welcoming in the artistic and different.

As I grew up, I fought against the unusual and pined for the normative. The image projected in after-school specials felt safe, good, and desirable.

As my mom continued her journey into the esoteric and spiritual, it rang empty and false to me. She'd hang a dream catcher in the window, talk about spirit guides, and then get drunk on a bottle of wine. Intuition got tossed aside with the other symbols my mom represented and I rejected. Addiction felt incongruent with the enlightened realm, so I chalked her spiritual questing up as another Fool card added to the tarot deck. I shut myself off from the ethereal because it felt like my mom's hippie shit, and I really missed out. I've spent a good chunk of my life being unaware of my intuition.

Disregarding intuition isn't just a result of my upbringing but of our culture. Western society favors logic, the mind, and the rational, and it often dismisses the felt sense—that which cannot be quantified but is felt in our bodies. The expression "trust your gut" is commonly accepted, but most of us don't know how to put these words into action. We're unaware of how to feel into the body and trust what it tells us.

Intuition is a felt sense. It's defined as the "ability to know something without analytic reasoning, bridging the gap between the conscious and nonconscious parts of our mind."[1] People intuit differently. Intuition is experienced through the senses, whether seeing images with an inner eye (clairvoyance), hearing an inner voice (clairaudience), experiencing strong bodily sensations (clairsentience), or receiving an immediate download (claircognizance). It can be both direct, where the message might be clear and literal, and indirect, where it may be symbolic.[2]

Whenever you get that internal *hell no* or full-body *yes*, it takes a beat for your brain to evaluate why you're feeling that way, because intuition works faster and sometimes more reliably than the conscious mind. Albert Einstein once told a friend, "All great achievements of science must start from intuitive knowledge... At times I feel certain I am right while not knowing the reason."[3]

When you approach a decision intuitively, your brain and gut work together, quickly pulling from your memories, past experiences, needs, and preferences and then makes the wisest decision given the context.[4] This instinctual mind-body response is why intuition is called a gut feeling, a hunch, or as the Navy SEALs puts it, a *spidey sense*. The US Navy invested millions of dollars to help their Seals develop and use intuition in high-stakes situations.[5] Intuition is a powerful survival asset.

Tuning into intuition requires us to understand what it *is* and what it is *not* and distinguish between inner senses. For many, tuning in means identifying the voices within. I hear these voices inside my head, and I bet you do too. The different voices can be jumbled and indistinguishable. Before coaching certification, I was a noob at discerning one voice from another, like a wine rookie unable to tell the difference between grapes from Burgundy or Bordeaux. Turns out that humans have access to intuition *and* well-developed inner saboteurs. Simply being aware of these voices is empowering. We can learn how to identify, strengthen, or weaken them, and we can choose which ones we listen to (huzzah!).

Choice is only possible when we are aware of the options. According to Shirzad Chamine, *New York Times* best-selling author of *Positive Intelligence* and faculty at Stanford and Yale Business Schools, there are ten inner saboteurs that can reside in the human mind, including the judge, the victim, and the hyper-achiever.[6] We develop inner saboteurs during childhood as a coping strategy to help us survive perceived or real threats. Most of these inner saboteurs are highly sophisticated mechanisms that outran their due date. Instead of keeping us safe as adults, they stop us from growing and opening up to what's possible. They keep us curled in a fetal position.

My main saboteur is the judge. According to research, the judge is the head honcho saboteur we all possess.[7] The judge chooses saboteur sidekicks for her stay-small-and-stay-safe mission. Mine rolls with the controller, an anxiety-based inner saboteur who needs to take charge. Together, they wrangle me into submission. That saboteur's voice gets *really* loud when we're on the cusp of big change, but it can also be insidious and leak into the everyday. We must learn to recognize it.

After years of tuning and practicing, I hear when my clients' saboteurs have entered the room. The tone, cadence, and speed of their voices change. Often, it feels like a jealous Debbie Downer blowing out the birthday candles before you do, peeing in your Cocoa Puffs, and generally raining on your parade. Just acknowledging the saboteur's presence is enough to remove the initial sting.

I ask my clients if they notice who just huffed and puffed into our space, what might have led to its arrival, and how they want to be with it. When I bring it to their attention, they are able to see it and identify its defining characteristics. This recognizability, a police sketch, helps them spot it when it pops up again. Not to demonize or vilify it, more like a "Hey there, it's you again. Thanks for trying to keep me safe, but I got this. We're good."

Let's normalize the saboteur showing up to crash the party uninvited without flowers or a bottle of wine—but bearing the gift of insight. Instead of obeying its demands, get curious instead. *What's activating it now?* Usually, there is a frightening desire or situation that reminds you of when an adult who had power over you as a child set limits. *What does it sound like?* Does it sound like your third grade teacher, Mrs. Wilson? A gruff sanitary worker from Yonkers? A nasal Jewish grandmother wagging a finger? Or someone else? *What happens in your body when this voice comes online?* Do you tense up? Does your throat close, shoulders crunch, or breath get shallow? Is the voice high-pitched or a grumbly rumble? *What circumstances does it love waltzing into?* Its appearance is an invitation to activate your curiosity, not criticize yourself.

Often, it is easier to recognize something by seeing what it is *not*. Your inner wise one, your spidey sense, or your intuition is not anything like the cagey, high-strung, critical saboteur. Your intuition speaks an entirely different language. It uses symbols, the body, colors, images, and words whispered in a firm but concise voice.

My intuition speaks to me in dreams, in words, and a felt sense in the form of full-body chills. Sometimes, when a client is speaking, I get the chills out of nowhere. I stop and share what I physically feel and ask what they feel or to repeat what they just shared. My intuition doesn't get to be right or wrong; it just is. Messages get lost in translation from gut to mouth. It can be challenging to translate a felt sense into words, so being unattached to how the message is received, remembering it is just an offering, is key to following whatever trail the client is moved to explore.

Your body is a gateway to intuition. Sometimes, the origin of the feeling is difficult to source. You just know. You just feel it. Trusting the feeling is key. Otherwise, you won't act on the information your gut is giving you.

A few months after my mother died suddenly, my husband and I went to Stockholm for my young cousin's baptism. My husband and I were the only people outside of my cousin's immediate family who flew in for the event. We were all out to dinner, and for the entire evening, something felt really off. I couldn't kick the feeling, especially around my aunt, the matriarch of the family. No one did anything I could point to, but something felt wrong in my bones.

Later, when we were back at the hotel, I turned to Teddy and said, "I feel insecure and weird, like we weren't wanted or something. I don't know, maybe I'm just being sensitive. Something felt really off."

"I didn't get that impression," he replied. "But if that's how you feel, trust it."

I escaped the uncomfortable feeling by curling under the white starched hotel sheet, taking a bite of a Swedish cardamom bun, and watching an episode of *Love Island*. The next morning, Teddy and I were eating brunch at the hotel with my aunt, preparing for another day in Stockholm. My aunt leaned over the table and told me in French, so my Danish husband couldn't follow, a piece of croissant flapping on her bottom lip, that we were taking time from her—precious time she intended to spend with her son, new grandson, and her other children. We were no longer welcome to join them on our last day in Stockholm. Gutted and stunned, my entrails spread over eggshells and coffee grains, I curtly got up from the table. We took the train back to Copenhagen early, and given my open wound of a heart, I cried the entire trip home.

Later, I spoke to my therapist about the situation. "Well, if anything, this confirms you can and should trust your gut," she said. "No need to question it again." She was right. This situation did confirm that I can trust my gut. I won't doubt the feeling in the future, regardless the lack of hard external evidence or "proof."

Besides leading to early train departures (guiding you in the right direction for *you*) intuition plays a critical role in the creative process. Celebrated mathematicians, scientists, and artists often say that trusting their gut feeling plays a big part in their creative discoveries.[8] Steve Jobs, a leading creative figure in recent history, heavily relied on intuition for his innovative ideas.[9] According to research, a creator who trusts their "hunches" about the unknown is more likely to develop a surprising solution rather than a predictable one. "Because there are no objective rules on how to reach a solution to a creative problem, a combinational explosion of possible choices occurs," and "relying on intuition is a common tool for coping with such a complex and noisy environment."[10]

In a study exploring the creative culinary process, a theme of intuition emerged during interviews with renowned European chefs. A key finding was the significant role of intuition in both generating and evaluating culinary ideas. These chefs reported experiencing two types of intuition: intuitive insight, where they mentally combine ingredients and develop a gut feeling about which combination should be tested; and intuitive judgment for evaluating the viability of their ideas.[11]

"A hunch is creativity trying to tell you something."[12]

—Frank Capra

Whether you're trying to decide if you should turn right or left or add miso or ginger to a recipe, or you're in the midst of building a business, cracking a brief, or developing a piece of art, intuition plays a critical role. It guides you to find *your* answers and craft your original, inimitable work. Intuition is a connection to something within and beyond that is not quantifiable, logical, or put-your-finger-on-it-able. It requires trust and an ability to feel into yourself and your open channel.

The answer is not out there but in here. Or even more accurately, your answer is where *in here* and *out there* meet. Learning how to write your own script and read from it means developing the capacity to tune into your intuition.

Let's hash it out

I get the craving to *just know* already. I spent years looking for answers *out there*. I searched for my answers at the bottom of a martini glass swimming with the olive, under a palm tree in Sri Lanka, inside someone's bruised heart, and in the pages of books. Someone must know! Yes, someone does know, and that someone was me.

The way to discover *your* right answers is through your body. You feel into it. I can hear your "WTF" whisper. I get it. We've been taught that knowing starts and ends with the mind: the logical, analytical, and reasonable. We've even gendered knowledge, assigning the rational as masculine and the irrational or "intuitive" as feminine. We shame intuition ("You're so woo") and the not-easily quantifiable. This has kept us from accessing our most powerful guide and resource—the illusive and felt "gut."

Learn how to listen to your own voice (so you can create from it).

Tapping into intuition will look different to different people, but it starts with meeting yourself daily. For me, that looks like meditating, free-writing or journaling, going for walks, moving my body, capturing my dreams, and stopping to check in with myself when feelings or sensations arise. I build trust with my inner guide, and I do that by listening when she speaks, whether somatically, as a felt sense in the body or as a clear, concise, soft but insisting voice. I pay attention to my gut vibes and feels, and I sit with them (on my good days).

I am in the process of breaking free from the belief that intuition is woo-woo hippie shit. I'm embracing the mystery, with the beautiful admission that I don't know, so why not experiment? I took an intuitive tarot card reading course that taught me to ignore the little pamphlet and trust what I see and feel instead. It's funny how often I question my interpretation of the cards. *You're probably just seeing what you want to see* is the usual saboteur line. But I get a gut feeling about the cards every single time. I am learning to trust these hunches, even if I don't understand them. Tarot is a land of lush symbolism, an intuitive language. And in the spirit of my mother, it flips the bird at conventional sources of external wisdom. Because you don't need to know it. You just need to feel it.

Fieldwork

Explore different ways of accessing your intuition, opening to this channel, and like a muscle, working it out. Before attempting any of these suggestions, give yourself *full permission* to trust that inner wise voice or feeling.

Get curious about how your intuition speaks to you. Is it:
- An inner voice—What are its qualities, characteristics, or tone?
- A felt sense—How does it manifest in your body? What does it feel like, and where do you feel it?
- An image, color, or visual in your mind—What shape or color does it take?
- Or something else entirely?

Experiment with different ways to access your gut feelings. Some food for hunches can be to:
- Sit quietly, daydream, chill, or calm the mind through meditation.
- Keep a journal by your bed. Ask a question before you go to sleep and see what you wake up with.
- Freewrite or draw in liminal spaces, either early in the morning or right before bed, and give your intuition room to bubble up.
- Use tarot or oracle cards and interpret the messages *before*—or without—consulting a guidebook.
- Tap into the wisdom of the body through repetitive movements—for example, running, dancing, or playing an instrument—and see what emerges.

Create evidence for your intuition so your logical mind—and inner saboteur—stop resisting it. Keep a notebook to jot down intuitive hits as they arise. In the moment, it often doesn't make sense, but in hindsight it does. This way, you generate evidence for the rational mind and reduce the resistance and friction that come up when intuition strikes and doesn't immediately "make sense."

sticky scripts

I'm a recovering nomad. As a kid, I moved from Spain to the Bowery, from the streets of Brooklyn to the beaches of San Juan, from the Financial District in Manhattan to the frozen streets of Montreal. I attended eight different schools. I'm not an army brat; my parents split when I was three, and my mother loved do-overs. Often, we didn't last more than a year in one place. I had to love and leave and not look back, because hanging on to the past stung like the high noon sun.

I'm fourteen, sitting on the beige futon in our twenty-first-floor apartment, one of the few skyscrapers in Ottawa, watching *Degrassi Junior High*. My mom looks up from the *New Yorker* magazine, pulls on her cigarette, and says, "We're moving to Montreal when the school year ends."

The striped La Baie wool blanket makes me sweat. "But it's just been a year. I love it here." I nervously pull my wavy thick hair into a scrunchie. "I don't want to move."

"I've been accepted to university in Montreal. Plus, your aunts are there, and I could use some help." Mom puts the magazine down and takes my hand. "You'll make new friends, just like you did here."

I snatch my hand away. My chest grows tight, tears threatening. "It's not the same! I don't want to make new friends. Maybe Sara's mom can take me in or I can figure something else out. I won't go." I run into my bedroom, slam the door, and throw myself on my bed.

Memories flood in, saltwater joining them: ice-skating on the world's largest natural ice skate rink, Le Rideau Canal, and stopping to eat beaver tails (fried dough and cinnamon) with Sara and Naomi. Laughing at each other's sugar mustaches. Kissing my first boyfriend,

Kemp Edwards, in the mall after he had just eaten a warm Mrs. Fields chocolate chip cookie. Wearing red lipstick for the first time and a bandana to the rock-themed high school party. Kemp joining in a leather jacket and slicked-back hair, dancing to Led Zeppelin's *Stairway to Heaven*, the heat of his hands on my waist, my arms around his neck for what feels like forever. Naomi, sitting on the floor outside the bathroom, telling me how to use a tampon. Sleepovers at Sara's sprawling house, eating Hot Pockets, listening to The Cure and playing Mansion Apartment Shack House, planning our futures together.

I was crushed like the cigarette my mother smashed into the ashtray. After we moved to Montreal, I tried to keep in touch, but attempting to shrink the distance made the gap ache more. When my friends either stopped picking up the phone or kept telling me stories I couldn't relate to ("You had to be there"), I saw their lives move on without me. Someone else was sitting at my desk or whacking balls into the pond at mini golf. My glimpse at a "normal" existence was wrenched away, and now, in Montreal, I feared I'd never have that feeling of belonging again.

I wouldn't allow myself to get stuck in the old places, unable to move onto the new. Why spend time talking on the phone to an old friend when sleepovers and mall hangs in real life are calling? I stopped looking back to move forward. My heart depended on slicing those ties with a Japanese blade. I taught myself how to leave—deeply connecting with others, even if just for short periods of time, and then letting go.

When things got tough, I learned how to create and live in different worlds. I'd lose myself in books, sitting on the carpet at Barnes & Noble on Sixth Street reading Judy Blume and Madeleine D'Engle. I'd write stories and conjure detailed visuals on what the future could hold. I cried when I found out Laura Ingalls from *Little House on the Prairie* would never really be my friend. I had a super active imagination, because sometimes, reality sucked. It kept me hopeful, optimistic, and generally happy. But I still felt very much at the mercy of outside forces.

These experiences imprinted some sticky beliefs:

Life is chaotic—a force to brace and fight against. When there was a wall, I would bang against it until it came down when I could have simply walked around it. This force served me well, until it didn't. Breaking walls was exhausting. It gave me bloody knuckles, achy biceps, and bruised shoulders.

Chaos and change were natural parts of life, so we became good friends and wore the same clothes. Chaos became what I knew, so when it was absent, I created it subconsciously. After graduating from Hunter College in New York City, I moved to Colombo, Sri Lanka, to work as a journalist. My friend Angie asked, "You're going where? To do what?" What was to be a three-month experience turned into two years of adventure. I left my life, boyfriend, and job behind and didn't look back—or bothered to tell said-boyfriend I had found someone else and ruthlessly moved on. Sooner or later, change would come, so I might as well enjoy what was there in the now.

Shape-shifting is a survival strategy. Frequently parenting myself led me to overcompensate on the responsibility front. My inner disciplinarian rode me to a gallop to make sure I maintained a 3.7 in undergrad and a 4.0 in grad school, even while drinking bottomless mimosas in a French bistro the morning after an all-nighter at an underground club, Danny Tenaglia spinning his wheels at Tunnel or Junior Vasquez at Twilo.

The escape—the steady release of steam on the dance floor, pupils dilated, sweat streaming, waves of euphoria rolling through my body, freedom vibrating along with the bass—was so sweet. Then I'd go to the bathroom, black doors covered with graffiti, glistening shirtless men with wild looks in their eyes, searching for the next bump, and gritty reality broke through the drug-enchanted forest. For a moment, at least.

When I did wake up, regret streamed in with the sunlight, along with a desperate need to not only find my bra on the floor but to collect the jagged pieces of yesterday into a cohesive memory. I knew I was more than this—more than a mouth that tasted like the bottom of an ashtray; more than headaches pounding like a landlord when the rent was long overdue; more than a girl mistaking dust for stars with lost boys and girls on an island within an island.

Happiness is around the next corner. I loved the musical *Annie* as a kid and would belt out "Tomorrow" at the top of my lungs and tap-dance to "It's the Hard-Knock Life." I'm six years old, dressed to the nines in a baby blue tutu littered with rhinestones and shiny black tap shoes. My mom's friend Isabelle arrives, and just as she walks through the front door, I take her hand, guiding her to the row of chairs I set up in the living room. My mom whispers to Isabelle, "Just go with it."

I turn my living room into a grand concert stage with my plastic red record player, bowing as the applause rings through our first floor townhouse apartment in Park Slope, Brooklyn. After the show is over, Mom and Isabelle move to the kitchen to drink *vin de table* and sample morbier, gruyère, and brie from the French bistro my mom waits tables at, *Raoul's* on Prince Street, and smoke a joint while Carly Simon's "You're So Vain" plays on the radio.

I bask in the glory of my stardom, oblivious to the party unfolding in the room next door. "Tomorrow" teaches me two things: If it is gray and rainy, all I have to do is dream of tomorrow. When the present got sharp as nails, when I'd bury my head in my knees in the closet feeling the ends of shirts playing with my hair, I'd project myself into the future and tell myself that tomorrow, there'll be sun. What was a very sophisticated and helpful coping mechanism designed by a kid outlasted its use and continued to be affirmed by capitalism: Happiness is hiding behind that next shiny thing.

I am safe in movement. Stopping or stillness required me to feel, to experience the backlog of pain. Every time I moved and morphed into the new tailored version of myself, I left parts of myself behind, a sock here, a high school jacket there. The freedom of fitting in anywhere cost shaving and shutting off parts of myself. If I stopped moving, I wouldn't be able to climb out of the hole I'd fallen in to.

Case in point, when I got divorced ten years ago, my first inclination was to move to Paris. What was circumstantial in my childhood became default. Curious about core beliefs, I asked my therapist, Christina, about how we rewrite past scripts that continue to direct our present behavior. I'm in her office. Her ivy plant, plush gray couch, and striped pillows make the space look cozy, not clinical.

"When people come to me, they usually have a problem, and it's often *not* from the present." That's how my relationship with Christina started. I wanted to run. I was running from one person to another, one place to another, one situation to another.

"We discovered running was your safety. When you stayed too long in the same place, you got stuck and needed another level of awareness to handle the situation of 'I don't need to run, I can face my fear, I can figure it out.'"

This restlessness wasn't a problem to begin with. After seeing Christina, it didn't take long for me to start asking, "How do I stop running? Do I even want to stop running?"

"It lived within you, and it was very demanding, unstable, and restless. We needed to identify where it came from before you could change it. You cannot change something you don't understand and can't understand something you didn't identify. Only then can you change it. Identify, understand, then change."

There's a reason I've been seeing this woman, my partner in healing, for over a decade. I dig a bit deeper, asking, "How does someone become aware of the core belief operating in the background?"

Christina leans back, plays with her necklace that says in Arabic "God opens the path in my life," and places her ginger tea on the coffee table.

"When you have a specific, problematic situation, ask yourself, *What's the belief behind it?* Often it's 'I'm not safe. I'm not good enough. I'm not worthy.' As a child, it might not have been a problem because you were taking care of yourself in survival mode, usually in relationship to parents, a problem, or a trauma. As a grown up, when the situation is no longer present but the core belief is, the response is still there. At some point, you don't hear it anymore. You're not aware of where it came from. Our coping strategies are responses to the core belief. If you believe you're not good enough, you should prove yourself—either by being very nice and a pleaser, by dominating, or by becoming a victim. We respond to the core belief by compensating for it."

The town hall bells ring, and light streams through the window. I add, "Once we become aware, we have the power to rewrite the belief and shift the behavior."

So, what does this have to do with creativity?

After working with partners, and most importantly working with myself, and then going down the coaching certification journey, I discovered my wounds are part of the unique medicine I bring to the world. And if transmuted, so are yours. I witnessed and helped people become aware of scripts and courageously rewrite their stories. A knot of beliefs and tug of intuition brought Justine to me as a client (now a dear friend). We're back on our old Zoom stomping grounds, her smooth caramel skin, cascading locks, and big grin in a neat box. I ask her what led her to rediscover her creativity.

"When we connected before I quit my job, a desire for freedom was calling me, and you helped me leap over the edge into my creativity. Yet creativity wasn't even in my mind, because I truly didn't believe I was a creative person. There's this concept in society that you're either a technical or a creative person, so I just never identified with it."

"So what helped you identify with being creative?"

"I started experimenting, trying new things, slowly unlocking parts of myself I didn't even know existed. I started by trying to create something small. The starting point has always been a project and wanting to bring something to life."

Justine's white fluff of a cat struts across the edge of her couch.

"Not believing I'm creative seems like such a strange thought now, because I wholeheartedly believe everyone is creative. I'll even go a step further: I think that's everyone's purpose. I feel like that's why so many people are feeling so lost, because they're not intentionally creating. I think we're all creating, even if we don't realize we're doing it. I understand now why my need for freedom was such a strong pull. I'm a creative person, and I need freedom in order to be the most creative version of myself."

So, what beliefs put you in the director's chair for your life production?

You are happening to life. What you believe, think, say, and do matters. It changes everything. Life is not a judgmental or parental force happening to you. It is benign, loving awareness happening through you, with you, and for you. You are the universe experiencing itself. You're life dancing with itself. Chassé, plié, jeté all day.

How you perceive the world becomes your experience of it. How you cultivate the relationship with yourself and life and heighten your self-awareness is the pathway to designing your reality and experience. If you believe people are shit, you'll call that forth because you're probably being shit yourself. If you believe people are inherently good, you'll experience a very different world.

"Whether you think you can, or you think you can't, you're right."[1]
—Henry Ford

You are 100 percent responsible for your life. You are an active agent and designer of your days. How can you architect your reality if you don't believe *you* are responsible for your experience? When you believe in your agency, creativity, and resourcefulness, you discover what might be possible (*anything*).

You already have it. Whatever you really want is accessible within. That's the only place it's available. It's not in the car, the salary increase, or the next trip. Sure, security and survival matter, but *that* thing you're really after is a feeling you have the power to create within yourself now. Freedom is a feeling, so are abundance and creativity, and that feeling is what you most likely really desire behind the "things" you want.

You are always at choice. There's only one thing you control in life: how you creatively respond to the challenges and circumstances you find yourself in. That's it. You always get to choose how you want to respond. Always. But you need to be aware of how you would like to respond to any given situation. It's not about the "perfect" response but a thoughtful and honest one. Sometimes, someone hits that big red button within, and your emotions go off like a jackpot at the slots, and that's okay. You're just practicing and discovering the game.

Don't let the past choose for you. Fuck autopilot. Someone honks their horn at you, you get to choose how you want to respond. Someone steals "your" parking spot, you get to choose how to respond. The love of your life breaks up with you, you get to choose how to respond. It's not judging the response in any way, shape, or form. It's simply making conscious choices. You can still scream into a pillow, cry oceans, kick inanimate objects, or eat a pint of Ben & Jerry's Cherry Garcia, honoring all your emotions. Just choose it consciously. Don't let past reflexes choose for you.

I am a recovering nomad who reacted to and then subconsciously created the chaos of life. As a black belt in unintentionally inciting life riots, I had no idea how to creatively and consciously direct my life. I needed to become aware of the past beliefs fueling my present behavior to rewrite my experience and future. Equipped with awareness and my favorite Pilot extra-fine blue pen, I started writing a new script and acting out the scenes. And so can you.

Fieldwork

You're in the driver's seat, setting the direction and speed: Where would you love to go? Allow yourself to imagine the most fulfilling destination. If you really let yourself go for it, where will you be in a year?

Now, read what you wrote. What limiting beliefs came up?

Some examples of commonly held dream-blocker beliefs are:
- Success is for other people, not for me.
- I'm too old to start something new.
- I don't deserve happiness/success/love.
- Things will never change.
- I can't fail.
- I should be able to make everyone happy.
- It's too late to change my path.
- I must be perfect.
- I don't have enough time/money/resources.
- It's selfish to put my needs first.
- I shouldn't rock the boat.
- If I'm not worrying, I'm not caring, or I'm not safe.
- Change is dangerous.
- I'm not a creative person.

Think back. What experiences led to these beliefs?

Now, what belief would you like to hold about yourself and life that would allow you to really go for it?

Some examples of limitless beliefs include:
- I am enough.
- Opportunities are abundant.
- I create positive change in my life.
- My past does not define my future.
- I am deserving of success, love, and happiness.
- Challenges are opportunities for growth.
- I have the power to shape my reality.
- My intuition is a trustworthy guide.
- There is always a solution.
- I am resilient and creatively ride the waves of life.
- I trust my process. I trust myself completely. I trust life completely.
- I am unattached to the outcome and create for the love of it.
- My ideas have the power to change the world.
- My story is worth telling.
- The entire universe is cheering for me, pom-poms galore.
- I am a creative badass who can do anything I put my heart and mind to.

How might you create evidence that this new belief is true *(that you really believe it)*?

Open your notes app or journal and document it.

between scripts

She stands in the kitchen. Bare feet on cold tiles. Ripped paper forms a reverse halo. Lips chapped, thirsty from tearing apart what once held her together. Eyes wide and blinking, she's in awe of how fast a story fragments. How, when observed, the familiar becomes alien. Without the script, she returns to an awkward adolescence. Between what is no longer and what is yet to arrive. A place between places. Sour bile burns her throat. Milk clumps in a carton on the counter. A rotting peach releases a sticky, yeasty scent. Her fingers grip the white Formica table, trying to hold on to something solid. Instead, electrons dance. The overhead light flickers and swings, the room coming in and out of view. Her breath, a steady rise and fall, anchors her. A black and white composition notebook comes into focus. Wiping the saliva from her lips with the back of her sleeve, she stumbles over to it, opens a blank page, and starts to script a whole new world.

fuck fear (do it anyway)

A sniper is on the loose. The cops bang on the door of my dad's loft on the Bowery on the Lower East Side, Manhattan. It is the 1980s, and drunks litter the street, spilling out of the men's shelter, punk wafting up from CBGB's, a homeless man steadied by a shopping cart hollers profanities and shakes his hand angrily at the injustice of the air, and artists like my father convert inexpensive lofts into studio spaces.

Officers need roof access to apprehend the sniper firing shots onto the street as he leaps from building to building like a villainous Spiderman. They climb the metal ladder to the skylight that leads to the roof, the same skylight that plays rain melodies. Heavy boots crush ivy plants. My dad watches the action, annoyed.

"Watch where you're stepping," Dad barks. I sense the frustration rolling off him like steam. The cops are oblivious of the ticking bomb shaking his head at the bottom of the stairs. I don't know what I was more scared of: my dad's pending explosion or the sniper. One is immediate, the other is still roof-hopping. My father rolls his eyes and emphatically sighs. "Come on, already," he grumbles as walkie-talkies beep and muffled voices sound above.

Afraid, I back up toward the wall, unsure of what to do with myself, searching for the code that will diffuse my father's anger. Nothing comes to mind, which makes my heart beat faster and fists clench. Luckily, the cops climb down, my father muttering, "Not the plants again!" and find their way to the door.

I read the energy in rooms (and bars), in people, especially my parents, and in different environments and cultures to smooth out the creases and make it okay. I think I have that power. If they're okay, I am okay. Right? This story brings the outside in, boundaries blurring.

Fear is insidious. It creeps into your system like a song you can't get out of your head. I think I am more fierce than I am because I have been put in situations way beyond my pay grade and age, yet I not only managed, but I managed well. According to research, a child with a complex trauma history may be easily triggered and react intensely. They often struggle with self-regulation and impulse control, making it hard to calm down or think before acting. This can lead to behavior that seems unpredictable, oppositional, and extreme, making them more likely to engage in high-risk behaviors.[1] I didn't know why, but I experienced this throughout my life.

Even though I see myself in the research, the fear of being labeled as traumatized or permanently damaged burns these diagnoses to a crisp. Reductive, simple explanations and categorizations ignore the different textures of my life, history, and experience; boxes that experts invite me into like a dog at a shelter, and I make a run for the door. It's hard to accept the idea that I do not determine myself, even harder to see myself reflected in child traumatic stress research.

As a love-struck teenager, I decided to visit my older chef boyfriend in the Bronx past midnight. The subway car empties as it climbs escalating street numbers, metal doors clanging violently, overhead lights flickering.

A young Latino draped in twisted gold chains, a flashy grill on his front teeth, jeans gathering into Timberland boots, and tattoos crawling up his neck boards the train and sits in front of me.

"What are you doing here at this time of night?" he asks. "It's dangerous to be alone."

If I wasn't scared before, I am shitting myself now. "Going to visit my boyfriend. I had no idea it would be so empty."

"Here." He hands me what looks like a piece of Big Red gum. "Open it carefully." I push the stick of gum upward, and a silver razor blade appears. "Keep it. You might need it. If anyone bothers you, tell them you're with Ñeta." He makes a sign with his fingers after placing his fist on his heart.

"Thanks so much. Really." I struggle to smile and remain seemingly calm while everything inside me is screaming, *Don't leave me here, please. Don't go, nice gang member. Stay with me.*

"No problem. You take care now," he says as he gets off at the next stop. I am left alone in a steel graffitied box, clutching the Big Red until my palm grows sweaty.

Who knew my guardian angel would be wearing a gold grill? When a gang member gives you a blade, tells you to be careful, and warns you about traveling on the subway late at night, you know you're in a dangerous place.

I survived it, even as I shook in sync with the metal cars. I fooled myself into thinking I was fearless. I was used to making moves while scared, because I often *had* to. As a young adult, I put myself in risky situations because it was what I knew. It made me feel alive, free, and invincible. All these years, I thought I had been so damn fearless, but underneath all the bravado was a little girl scared shitless—*who did it anyway.*

That little girl's fear was the fault line in my foundation. It created a wobbly hesitancy; an insecurity that appeared as I got older, which didn't track with my self-perception. When I needed to make big, bold moves, I felt shook and unsure. Fear has been following me incognito for most of my life. I got so used to its refrigerator hum, I didn't notice it was there.

There's nothing inherently wrong with fear. It's a useful emotion defined as the "anticipation of danger from a physically present threat (a grizzly bear in front of you)."[2] Unfortunately, our nervous systems can't tell the difference between a charging bear and a work deadline. When we *perceive* a threat, the brain sets off an alarm throughout the central nervous system, causing quick and shallow breaths, tense muscles, clenched fists, and dilated pupils.[3]

If we don't take a beat to calm the nervous system, we might find ourselves in a fear response from traffic jams, uncomfortable family dinner conversations, or financial stress. When fear becomes the unconscious driver, whether daring you to touch the flame or not get too close to the fire; when it becomes the master, and not the servant, *that's* when it becomes a problem. Sometimes, fear keeps you safe, and sometimes it blocks you, and you need to tell the difference between the two.

Feeling fear before traveling deep into the Bronx on the subway past midnight in the 1990s would have been helpful to listen to, but letting it stop me from going on the Trans-Siberian because I'm afraid of not finding a job despite receiving severance pay is harmful. As an adult, I can notice fear when it manifests in my body and assess if the fear response matches reality or if my nervous system is reacting to an old trigger. In other words, is this a fitting or appropriate response to the situation at hand? Do I need to take a few deep breaths, shake, or run in the other direction? Is my very survival at stake? Is Freddy Krueger ripping through my dreams, or am I about to jump toward my deepest desires into the unknown? Only I can tell the difference if I pause to consider it.

"Leap and the net will appear."[4]

—Julia Cameron

Fear is also a signal that you are in the growth zone. It screeches: *This is the ledge, the edge—back up, back up!* You're on the cusp of change, on the precipice, wind whipping strands of hair in your mouth. Maybe you're mid-flight, unsure of where you are because you're not *there* yet. It might feel like you're falling when you're actually flying. It is wildly uncomfortable, especially when you don't realize you're in the process of leveling up.

You know you're in the growth zone when you might be feeling lost, experiencing real discomfort, wrestling with self-doubt, and feeling excited about what's possible. It is precisely in *this* fertile creative place that anything is possible. You don't know what will emerge from the process because you are deep in it. It is new and unknown. You have never been here before. When you're experiencing mother-load growth spurts, often by your own design, you're throwing yourself out to sea, releasing yourself to the current. It feels uncomfortable because you have no idea where you'll wash up.

If you're in the weird in-between, remember: *You are a courageous, creative badass in the midst of wild growth.* Even if you are not where you want to be yet, if you are on the road, going and growing, you're going to feel alive. Despite not knowing much about Tony Robbins, one of his quotes feels like a universal truth. "Progress equals happiness."[5] My twist is "Growth equals fulfillment." Growth is uncomfortable—scary even. The universe is continuously expanding, and so are we, and this growth gives us tremendous satisfaction.

This doesn't mean there's no place for comfort in transformation. You flirt with your edges, rub shoulders against your borders, until you inch beyond them. Then, exhausted, you might retreat to the comfort of a pillow fort. At some point, when your nervous system is regulated and ready, as you build your capacity for bigger spaces, you return to the ledge. This time, you might jump.

Know this: Your dream will require you to get wildly uncomfortable. You might not know the difference between flying, flailing, and falling until you are in the air, and maybe you will be doing it all at once.

> *"If your dreams don't scare you, they're not big enough."*[6]
>
> —Ellen Johnson Sirleaf

Working as a creative director in a purpose-driven consultancy was super cushy and all good on paper. I judged award shows, worked with exciting clients using creativity for good, got a steady and handsome paycheck, but something more was calling me, sometimes even heckling me, throwing peanuts to get my attention. I wanted to see what I would build on my own, the ghost of what *could* be haunting me for years.

I muffled the voice of fear with a pillow over my head at night when a series of questions kept me up: *What would I do exactly? Where would I begin? What does the dream even look like? Will I survive? What if I don't?*

When I started an intense journey into coaching certification in 2021, my self-awareness grew. I became aware of the negative *what if* story and the pen in my hand. If I could write the "What if I fail?" fear script, I can also rewrite it to "What if I succeed?" I could flip the *what if* unknown horror show into a feel-good rom com.

Yet I was too scared to pull the trigger, stuck in my own negative *what-ifs* and lulled by the comfort of *good enough*. I had forgotten that nomadic girl who grew up among snipers and drunks, the teenager on the train—not only the survivor, but the brave thriver. Still, I was unsure, complacent, and *comfortable*.

> *"Yesterday you said tomorrow."*[7]
>
> —Nike Ad

When my mother had a sudden stroke in 2021, I flew to Mexico during a global pandemic stunned, shattered, and in disbelief as I ran to catch connecting flights. Nothing could have prepared me to see my fiercely independent mother paralyzed and unable to speak. She seemed so small on the hospital bed. Yet when she was asleep, I imagined she'd wake up, and this would be one of her elaborate pranks. I hoped she'd snap out of death's grip, but it had fallen for the striking blonde, like so many before it, and wasn't about to let go.

I didn't want to let go either. How could the woman who brought me into this world, who knew me from the moment my head crowned out of her, be leaving? I tried to memorize her crescent nails, the curve of her chin, and the echo of her smoky, phlegmy, take-over-the-room laugh.

Her doctor kept warning me about her imminent death, giving me multiple chances to shake the contents of my heart out. Every time I thought it would be the last, I told her how much I loved her again and sang Tracy Chapman's "Fast Car" and Patsy Cline's "I Fall to Pieces." I found my way into her cot, listening to her fight for air, wrapping my fingers between hers.

When I came home, I read *The Five Invitations: Discovering What Death Can Teach Us About Living Fully*, written by Frank Ostaseski, cofounder of the Zen Hospice Project, who sat on the precipice of death with more than a thousand people.[8] I learned the body passes through the four elements as it surrenders to death: earth (the body gets heavy, numb, or immobile); water (the body swells); fire (fluctuating temperatures); and air (a lengthening of breath intervals).

I wished I knew this beforehand. Alone in the hospital in San Miguel de Allende, I had no hospice support, just nurses and a mostly absent doctor who checked vitals. No one explained what happens when a body dies and consciousness moves into the fifth element—space. I could have remained calmer when her temperature shot up, her breath seemed to stop, or her fingers doubled in size. Walking a parent home is a journey us lucky ones get to take. Watching her die made me realize that in the end, we lose everything.

Nothing mattered and everything mattered when I returned home from Mexico. I went on sick leave to the small, beautiful island of Samsø so I could grieve by the sea, shriek at the moon, dance to my mother's favorite songs, and hear her tell me the right way to dice an onion in the kitchen. I experienced the tidal wave of grief, the undertow pulling me to my knees, salt water washing over me. I discovered I could face my biggest fear with a badly bleeding heart. Yet, I was underwater, floating above the surreal reality of doing laundry and trying to plan my return to work at my boss's insistence.

I caught the best case of the fuck-its ever. My mom's death reminded me that I have one wild and precious life, and I get to decide what I want to do with it. I sobered to the reality of my own mortality. What did I *really* have to fear? Definitely not leaving my job and seeing what would happen if I channeled my creativity into building my own dream instead of someone else's. It's precisely because my time is finite that *not* doing it would be the frightening choice. Luckily, I had savings and a cushion. My survival wasn't at stake, but my sense of fulfillment and expansion were. So what was I going to do about it?

Fuck it. Fuck fear.

I'm jumping.

After three years of founding Kollektiv Studio, there are days when I just want to be *there* already; when I want it all to be crystal clear, not even one soap stain on the glass. Days when that fearful part of me trying to keep me safe wants me to move back to the known and figure it all out already; to board the next cruise ship, even though I hate cruises, just to know where I am. There are moments when I feel the ground beneath my feet, but more often than not, I can be found in a donut pool floatie in the Baltic Sea drifting under the light of my North Star.

Nothing feels more alive than embracing uncertainty and *not* ignoring its existence like one of the Heathers does to the less popular girls. Everything is uncertain. Anything can happen. You could lose your job, an air conditioner could fall on your head; your partner could get a diagnosis; you could trip and break your leg; you could win the lottery, connect with a game-changing partner, fall in love with someone waiting for the bus, or lose your mother. That's the beauty and terror of life.

We try so hard to erase this truth off the whiteboard, but the marks remain (that kid used a permanent marker). We create false security through routines and schedules to avoid the uncomfortable truth that life is uncertain, unknown, and uncontrollable. We hurry along on the commute seemingly oblivious to the fact that we're on a planet spinning across one of hundreds of billions of galaxies and have no idea how we got here really or where we're going after this earth trip.

> *"Let the mystery unfold."*
> —Dennis Ferman, senior teacher, Vipassana
> Meditation as taught by S. N. Goenka

This could either terrify you and keep you stockpiling Campbells soup like some Warhol art piece gone wrong or motivate your socks off and propel you to heights Icarus never dreamed of. Uncertainty is a portal to infinite possibilities, but you need to walk through it.

Your creative potential is shaped by your ability to stay in the unknown and uncertain growth zone. This is where *anything* is possible because nothing is fixed. It helps to recognize when you're in the chrysalis and then learn how to increase your capacity to be in this space. As a creative, learning how to regulate your nervous system is key to growth and expansion. Because if you're intentional, curious, and passionate, you'll find yourself in this leveling-up space more often than not.

The more you release into it, the more joy starts to flow, that feeling of aliveness permeates your bones, synchronicities start to occur, and serendipity follows. It makes life thrilling. Sometimes, all you need to do is allow yourself to be in it, to float, let the water carry you, feel the sun on your cheeks, and stare into the night sky wearing its Liberace outfit.

Learning to recognize when you're in the growth zone is part one of creative living. Writing a new story about fear and redefining your relationship to life is part two. You learn to recognize fear and choose trust instead. Trust in yourself and life. Trust you won't drown (you know how to swim or float). Trust when you intentionally enter the sea, the waves will carry you exactly where you need to go.

Notice the pattern and make a choice. It's the winter of 2023, and I turned into the Airbnb in Joshua Tree. The left side mirror of my Ford Edge rental car collides with the metal gate, sounding like a dozen Coke cans being crushed in the fist of a giant. Squeezing the beastly SUV into a tight driveway enclosed by a temperamental gate and breaking the side mirror was not the kick-off we were hoping for on our girls' reunited road trip. Not exactly cowboy pools, fire pits, and bleeding sunsets.

My anxiety peaks like a diabetic who just feasted on Cinnabons with extra icing at the mall. The glass splintered side mirror magnifies underlying anxieties. Thoughts come crashing through. *I've invested a lot of money in this trip. How much will this cost? What if I get in trouble? I'm falling behind in my business. What if this time off hurts my business? What if it risks my very survival?*

Spiraling irrational thoughts make me sweat through my natural Palo Santo deodorant. It takes a couple of hours to shake the fear off, like the sand gusting around Joshua trees, and reconnect to my center and what matters. I remember where I am—in the desert, one of my favorite places to be. The wild expansiveness makes me feel free, open, and filled with effervescent possibilities. I remember who I'm with, a dear friend I've known and loved for over twenty years. I'm lucky. This is good. This is a deeply nourishing miso ramen soup on a blustery winter's night type of trip.

So fuck the side mirror. And fuck fear (again). Leaning into trust instead of being fueled by fear is not *just* a belief, an affirmation, or a bedtime story that makes you feel better or safer spinning on this rock in the middle of the Milky Way. It is a way of being. It's behavioral—a verb, not a noun. Each action you take is a demonstration of trust or an act of fear. Even though I crush hard on my business, I doubt I'll regret not working more when my number gets called and it's time to exit stage left. But I *would* regret not spending time with people I love dearly.

My daily note to self is "I'm not just building a business, I'm designing a life." And my business needs to support the juiciest vision of life I have—today and tomorrow. I need to *live* that, not just say it. It's not easy to release the wheel (doing) and trust the direction (being). You get used to momentum, to speed, and it can feel like losing or falling behind when you ease up. Until you check yourself, which I do frequently, stepping back, eyeballing the big picture, and reminding myself if my business doesn't create space for me to focus on what really matters then I'm building a prison, not a palace.

This is living creatively. Things trip you up, and the universe gives you a chance to practice choosing trust. Fear swaggers into the room channeling Patrick Swayze in *Dirty Dancing*, and you choose to dance on your own. The challenge becomes a growth opportunity. You become aware of old patterns that no longer serve (mine is gripping and grinding fueled by camouflaged fear) and make a conscious shift to moving with trust through life. First, awareness, which might be theoretical. *I don't want to be in fear's 1990's WWF Jake the Snake Roberts chokehold. I want to move with ease and trust with life.* Great. Now what?

It needs to be applied. I like to think of it as proof of belief. *See, universe? I'm not just talking jazz, I really do trust.* That's integrity at play, not because you're trying to game the system and get the narrow version of what you want, but because you trust what's coming for you is what you need. Having a little faith, you're also showing yourself—even as you clench your jaw, red-faced before the bungee jump because you're not that pumped to throw yourself off a cliff but do it anyway because it swings you in the direction of your dreams—that you trust yourself and life. You show yourself you can do hard things.

You're building that muscle every time you do something that scares you in the name of *that* life, business, or creation you're beautifully and intentionally designing. **So, whatever you are choosing to believe, also choose to apply and practice.** That's how you create new neural pathways, fresh snow falling on deep grooves, inviting you to take the powdery, trackless, new path. That's the road to change.

After the shattered mirror and avalanche of anxious thoughts, the white-knuckled grip slowly released and the blood ran through my fingers again. Simply being aware of the feeling helped shift my belief and behavior. It was visceral and high contrast—from panties in a tight twist to a weightless au natural. I went from being a hot anxious mess to a calm Bruce Lee flowing like water in a matter of hours. I did that, and so can you.

You'll need to become aware of fear, understand its signal, discover what story fuels it, and reframe that narrative to build the dream, the venture, the brand, the art, the poem, the book, or the business. Fear is a natural part of our existence. Its presence is a message you can decipher and use. *Is there something that needs healing or rewiring, or is it simply an indication that I'm in the growth zone? Is it pointing to a script that needs to be flipped? Or is there a bear I need to run from?*

Ultimately, when *creating* something new, when stretching in the direction of what you really want, when in the middle of transformation, fear will appear. It might try to take the wheel, thinking you're about to reenact a *Thelma & Louise* scene. Desperate, it might incessantly scream "Shotgun!" but you can put it in the backseat, or even the trunk, where it belongs. No fiddling with radio dials, no attempting to thwart the itinerary, but neatly buckled up in the back, along for the ride.

Pull up a chair

Your creative growth depends on your capacity to be in uncertainty. Creativity, by nature, requires not knowing. You're creating something new or making it in a way that's new to you, so by default, it will be unknown and uncertain. The mind doesn't vibe with uncertainty. In fact, it will do whatever it can, even creating false evidence and flashy attention-sucking stories, to keep you in the feeling of *knowing* through similar patterns and behaviors. This shrinks possibilities and limits our creativity.

Creativity requires us to be uncertain, release attachment to outcomes, and create ideas without knowing what they will become. You can't see what you haven't created yet. It's scary not to know. So, it's helpful to remember that uncertainty is not only the realm of knee-knocking angst but also endless possibilities.

The hard truth is that we're always in uncertainty, so we design systems and structures that make us feel safe in it. When you're at the DMV, earning a steady paycheck, doing laundry, buying cat food, or attending a PTA meeting, it's easy to forget you will expire at some unknown date in the future. This scaffolding might keep us feeling certain and "safe," but it also keeps us small, narrows our aperture, and sucks the juice out of this wild life experience, throwing its rind on the ground with dramatic emphasis.

Uncertainty is exactly what we need to create, come alive, and feel the blood pumping through our veins even as we ask our partner, once again, what we should make for dinner. Usually, a big life event changes the routine channel. It shakes us by the shoulders, sticks our noses in the fragile, tenuous, and fleeting beauty of life, and gives us the courage to move into uncertain but meaningful spaces.

Entrepreneurship created the gym that helped me strengthen my uncertainty muscle. When I launched Kollektiv Studio, I didn't know what I was building, where clients would come from, or when the next paycheck might arrive. I had no idea how it would turn out—and still don't. But I had a vision, a purpose, and an unquenchable thirst and gut pull that this was where I was supposed to be, and it was a nightlight in the dark. Coaching, being a coach, and getting coached helped loads.

The more I leaned into the unknown, trusting myself and life, the more I experienced the fun and thrilling part of uncertainty. As I walked into big, expansive, open spaces, I strengthened my ability to stay in uncertainty, one step at a time, taking up more space and entering even bigger, grander rooms in the Italian villa of my life.

The answers are revealed during the creation process, *not* before you begin. This sounds logical, yet most of us want to know how it will turn out before we start creating, which is like wanting to know how a movie ends before we watch it, and no one likes spoilers.

If you wait until you know before you create or leap, you'll be waiting a long time. That's the essence of creativity: not knowing what it will become but doing it anyway because you are being called to it. Even when the message is like a game of banana phone, you answer anyway. You got this one precious life, so why wouldn't you?

As neuroscientist Beau Lotto says, "Can you think of one thing that you discovered in your life that didn't begin with not knowing?...How could you discover it if you already knew it? You had to not know it first. Not knowing is a wonderful, wonderful thing. And there are ways of being, and processes by which we cannot just deal with uncertainty, but thrive because of it."[9]

I've been asking myself how to stay in uncertainty because I've discovered that's the real creative flex. So far, I've come up with five uncertainty capacity builders.

1. **Trust, faith, or belief**—pick your antidote. When I trust life, I believe whatever life throws at me is in service of my growth. It might not feel good at the time, but it is something I need to learn to expand; that's the nature of the universe, after all. I might not understand it now, but I can trust it's here for a reason. When I embody this belief, it invites me to stay in uncertain spaces with more ease.

2. **The reaper.** Reminding myself that I'm going to die inspires me to really live, which means taking chances, showing up, being visible, taking up space, giving less fucks, being vulnerable, jumping and leaping, and really going for it.

3. **Your unique spice.** I could have chosen any number of incarnations, but I selected Pia. There's a reason I won the earth lottery, and my desires are mine. The universe, a.k.a. my intuition, whispers directions in my ear if I get silent enough to hear them. When I stop trying to control things, I flow with the current of life and see where it takes me.

4. **The human collective.** We're not alone in it. We're in this crazy celestial experience together. We can help each other be in uncertainty without the addiction to busy work and any number of distractions that help us avoid our fragile existence. Imagine what happens when we admit we don't know, get curious, and develop a deeper relationship with uncertainty together?

5. **Reconnect to the thrill of it.** With each big leap into the unknown, I've felt more alive and excited, which hushes the fear (shhhh, already). It creates evidence for my uncertainty-averse mind that I can expand into the unknown and not die (she's a real drama queen). It makes not knowing, uncertainty, and, most importantly, creation fun—most of the time.

Every new expansive step toward a creative life requires you to be with and in the uncertain unknown. Knowing you can trust yourself, life, and who you get to become in the creative process is solid gold certainty. It's the beam we can lean against in a room without walls.

Fieldwork

Ask yourself these questions and journal or voice note the responses:
- What am I letting go of?
- What am I inviting in?

Practice regulating your nervous system when you're in the unknown. Get comfortable in discomfort, or at least increase your capacity to be in it. Some inspiration:
- Breath work. Box breathing is a great way to calm and regulate your nervous system. Breathe in, counting to four slowly. Feel the air entering your lungs. Hold your breath for four seconds. Slowly exhale through your mouth for four seconds. Repeat this cycle for at least five minutes to get the full effect. Fun fact: The Navy SEALs use box breathing to quickly get the nervous system under control in high-stakes situations.[10]
- Create and repeat affirmations as you brush your teeth twice a day that ground you in the present and all that is here, right now. Some food for thought: *I trust myself completely. I trust life completely. I am grateful for all that I am and all that I have. It's safe to build my dream.*

Want a few more ways to soothe your system? Try these:
- Walk in nature.
- Journal and freewrite.
- Pet your dog or cat.
- Shake it out (move your body).
- Get and give hugs.

hungry
a poem for A-types

Clutching onto a desired outcome
like your LVH bag in the Bronx
chokes your creativity,
draws unwanted attention
from the inner critic rolling a toothpick
in his mouth across the street.

Expecting to see
what is being made
before it is done
is wanting dinner to be ready
while you're still preparing the meal.
Creativity's not a Pop-Tart,
she's the glee of Julia Child
as she adds more wine to the coq au vin.

When the idea is fully baked,
it needs to be served to the world.
No matter how you plate it,
people will either love or hate it.
Or worse, not even glance at your dish
glistening like ducks in a Chinatown window.

Trying to control how an idea is received
is a bad deal made in a cheap motel
smelling like damp cigarettes and bleach.
Ideas murdered, their blood staining
starched sheets, the room now
the odor of iron and expired milk dreams.

Make art your thirst trap for the G-O-D
your way to connect to twenty-one grams
to offer medicine to the wounded
to map constellations with beauty marks
to leave a trace of the recipe
you're still making.

Savor the flavor of the being-made
orange glazed sweet and sour sauce
on top of nothing yet.

la dolce far niente is doing something

New York City was a strange parent. I was raised on the milk of a city with insomnia. Its amped-up heartbeat; scent of sugar-roasted nuts, hot dogs, and sauerkraut; and its siren song of pulsing metal, possibilities, and concrete all wrapped me in a blanket.

When I was twelve years old, my father and I walked through the streets of Chinatown, glazed orange ducks in the windows, to pick up fresh mozzarella in Little Italy. My father barked convincingly like a rottweiler to part the crowds, pulling me by the tricep to get through the throngs, fast. He gave a recurring speech whenever my mom made him wait, which was often when it was her turn to pick me up. "All a man's got is his time. You should never rob him of it." Minutes mattered; seconds counted. Speed was paramount. Movement became familiar and safe.

It's easy to spot a New Yorker, dodging and weaving through crowds. I calculate the ways to save minutes throughout a day, finding the exact car on the subway platform that drops me off at the closest exit to wherever I am going. I speak fast and direct. There's no time for miscommunication, subtly, or innuendos. I walk with my eyes narrowed to a tight aperture.

There are parts of New York City I've never seen because I'm in a rush. It took a gregarious ginger Scottish professor wearing flannel and tweed, with an accent that made me sit in the front row and pay close attention, to show me. I enrolled in a master's social anthropology class about New York City taught by Mr. Scottish, which involved day trips around the city and evening trips to the Irish pub.

On one of our tours of Manhattan, he told us to look up at the theater unfolding above. I noticed the gargoyles, dragons projecting out of buildings and ogre-looking creatures holding a book or a hammer. I'm enchanted and surprised by the fantasy world above my head, thinking, *How did I miss this?* They glared at oblivious pedestrians, lost in the speed game, never stopping to look up.

During my twenties, my heartbeat matched the pulse of the city. Me and the city, we're at eye-level. It sends a steady stream of invitations— from hotel rooftop parties to after-hour clubs, from experimental opera to poetry slams—and I curtsy and accept.

Manhattan is a short ride on the subway over the Fifty-ninth Street Bridge from my apartment in Astoria. Something happens when I enter the quieter expanse of Queens, with its shorter and smaller buildings. It lulls me into staying home, not wanting to leave my apartment again. I got into the habit of staying in Manhattan, moving from classes to dinners to parties. I change into my evening attire at Urban Outfitters, ready for the transition to the city at night, which is never one place, one party, but a series of stacked and beautifully escalating experiences.

I meet friends at a Moroccan-themed lounge on the Lower West Side. It's darkly lit, candles flickering, the scent of Oud and sweat joining the beat of live drummers. A giant watermelon glistens on top of a long mahogany bar backlit by rows of bottles. The bartender scoops pink flesh into high-ball glasses, mixes it with ice and Ketel One vodka, and hands it to me. I drink it like fruit punch, dance, and sweat until the moment fades and it's time for the next one.

We head to a private party in a penthouse with floor-to-ceiling windows overlooking the Williamsburg Bridge. We move from one scene to the next, not wanting the electricity to fade and be left in the dark. We chase the newness, the charge, and leave what came before behind, tossed aside like the cigarette I flicked on the street, and don't look back.

This rhythm becomes part of me. I move frequently and fast.

It's no wonder I end up working in creative agencies. It's 2007, and I start working at a brand communication agency in London. It's my first agency job. The team is tasked with coming up with ideas to help our client make headlines and raise awareness of their brand and new product. Ideas flow through me, spilling into the room and onto the white board. I spitball as we build on each other's ideas. Everything feels possible and like fun, not work. *I can't believe I get paid for this,* I think. In that carpeted meeting room on Marylebone Road, with its Post-its, sketch pads, and colored markers, I feel at home.

We work with multiple clients simultaneously and have a limited amount of time and budget to solve any given commercial challenge. The deadline is almost always "Yesterday," said with an apologetic smile. It's 8:00 p.m., and I am still at my desk, trying to take the work to the next level, when my manager passes by on his way out.

"You'll never get it all done," he says, "no matter how late you stay. Your job is to do your best with what you got in the time you have." Clients inevitably want out-of-the-box, breakthrough ideas fast and within a limited budget. Creating a real innovative solution requires us to stay in the problem, not try to find the fastest way out of it, but clients won't pay for that.

This push for getting it done faster, cheaper, better is not only pervasive in the agency world; it extends to other industries and work generally. We are geared to believe more is better and faster is the way to success. Profitability is a twenty-four-seven blood, sweat, and tears job not for the fainthearted. A former client once told me that many companies, including her own, hire insecure overachievers because they know what they'll get from them: everything. Tireless dedication to proving themselves through work, accolades, and titles, and they will trade their time for it—and eventually burn out.

Creativity thrives in constraints but wilts when not given enough space.

There is a place for passionate, focused, and intense work, but often what fuels work into overdrive is fear: the fear of not making it, failing, falling behind, being of little consequence, and not surviving.

What if we're getting it very wrong? That busyness doesn't guarantee success but moves us further away from fully inhabiting and enjoying this life and distances us from our creative birthright? Creativity doesn't thrive in cubicles or production lines. Creativity is not something you squeeze in between meetings or show up saddled with expectation and a desired speed to achieve a very specific outcome. It needs breaks, room to wander, trust, and releasing the illusion of control.

Ask yourself: What would happen if I allowed space for ideas to emerge and creativity to run wild, making random but powerful connections through the subconscious at play? Perhaps most importantly, what do I miss, what is blurring by, when I move at the speed of a Japanese bullet train through life?

What if my creative genius (and yours) lives on the other side of rest?

According to neuroscience research, unleashing our creative potential requires creating space to daydream, wander, and rest to tap into a different aspect of our brain—the default mode network (DMN). The DMN is a large-scale network of interconnected brain regions that are active when you are at rest or not focused on the outside world. Basically, it is the system in your brain that does the thinking when you're not thinking. When the prefrontal cortex quiets down, and we're not focusing on goal-oriented tasks, the brain's default mode network kicks in.[1]

The DMN is the brain's resting-state circuitry that activates during downtime, when you're zoning out. "Downtime," or unstructured time, is not watching Netflix or even reading a book. It is when you have no agenda, no plan, no task to check off, and no intention—or the intention to be unintentional.[2]

It is activated when we're not focusing on anything specific, allowing the mind to wander or marinate in memories, ideas, and emotions. A study found that positive, constructive daydreaming—"characterized by planning, pleasant thoughts, vivid and wishful imagery, and curiosity"—is associated with activity in the default mode network and creativity. "The default mode network seems to be an important source of creativity, and it's decidedly associated with mind-wandering," says Jonathan Schooler, a psychological scientist at the University of California, Santa Barbara.[3]

Scientists have since found mind-wandering to be crucial for triggering insights. Thomas Edison routinely let his mind drift, hoping dots would connect and new ideas would take shape. He captured these fleeting thoughts in a notebook, believing they were often creative. Research confirms what Edison knew: Giving the mind space to roam can lead to breakthroughs.[4]

"Moments before an insight, we unfocus visually and mentally to enable an idea to bubble to the surface."[5] In other words, we create space for ideas to emerge by not forcing, pushing, demanding, or doing anything except just being. How awesome is that? Not so awesome if you're hardwired to *do*. Given how critical the DMN is for creativity, it is surprising we don't prioritize practices that activate it.

The DMN helps you combine information in different ways and simulate possibilities. When you are not actively working on a problem, the brain keeps spinning, restructuring elements of the problem, and reshuffling pieces, and then something clicks, explains Roger Beaty, director of the Cognitive Neuroscience of Creativity Lab at Penn State University. This is often referred to as "the incubation effect," which happens when you spend time away from a particular problem and "your mind has the chance to wander and generate novel ideas through unconscious associative processes."[6]

Creativity relies on more than just the DMN. It's a dynamic dance between spontaneous and deliberate thought. Several creativity researchers argue that creativity depends on the interaction between the default and control networks. DMN activity has been characterized as "'spontaneous' thought and the activity of the control network as 'deliberate' thought." The mind continuously moves between the world outside and the inner world of imagination.[7] Neuroscientist Nancy C. Andreasen's study on creativity reinforces this interplay: Almost all her subjects reported "eureka" moments after long periods of preparation and incubation, often striking when the mind was relaxed—in a state she calls "REST" (random episodic silent thought), also known as the default state.[8]

Graham Wallas was the first to create an overview of the creative process in his book *The Art of Thought* from 1926.[9] Wallas showed, as does my fifteen-plus-year creative career, that the creative process has four stages:

1. Preparation (knowledge gathering)
2. Incubation (a process that happens when you're *not* focused on the task)
3. Illumination (creative idea flashes)
4. Verification (creative ideas are evaluated)

"You need that exploratory aspect of idea generation in order to be creative, but you need other parts of your brain to pick an idea, evaluate its viability, and implement it in the real world," explains Rex Jung, a neuropsychologist at the University of New Mexico in Albuquerque. "It's an interplay or dance between the default mode network and the cognitive control network that allows you to generate a creative idea then implement it effectively."[10]

Yet, we tend to over-prioritize preparation and verification and undervalue incubation and illumination. Research and knowledge gathering and evaluating the work takes precedence. This feels important since it can be easily quantified, proven, and demonstrated. It fits into the busy, productive, fast-paced box, so it must be valuable. It is acceptable to create time in your calendar for research or deck preparation, but daydreaming or naps, not so much. There is no job number for that.

"People always get surprised when they realize they get interesting, novel ideas at unexpected times," says Kalina Christoff, a cognitive neuroscientist at the University of British Columbia in Vancouver, "because our cultural narrative tells us we should do it through hard work. It's a pretty universal human experience."[11]

Most of our time is spent preparing and verifying. No wonder many of us are all gunked up, claiming we're not the creative type. There's no space for rest, mind-wandering, and doing nothing with no intention or desired outcome. We're squeezing the juice out of our creativity and wondering why our idea well is dry. We put demands on the ideas, expectations (even worse). The idea needs to rise immediately and be useful. But that's not how it works. We need to honor all parts of the creative process.

What if the next level of our creative genius is found in the space of being, daydreaming, and slowing down? I got neuroscience backing this theory. So, how do we teach ourselves how to move differently in the world and with our creativity?

It starts with learning how to feel safe in stillness. If I want to create a different future, one where I get to make animal shapes from passing clouds, where my creativity soars to unfathomable heights in the clearing, where I sway like underwater algae through life, and my drive doesn't rule me but I channel and direct it when needed, I must move differently. I have to wean myself off that sweet rush of New York City milk and find my own trust-filled pace and rhythm; a musical score I get to write and produce instead of following someone else's track. I get to reconnect to the beat in my veins, reclaim my movement, and give myself permission to rest and space out. My creativity depends on it—and so does yours.

Straight talk

We need to slow down to dream. Breaking can often feel scarier than speeding, because when we take our foot off the gas, we have to meet ourselves and feel. Dreaming is dangerous because it means having to look at where we are now and where we want to go. The space in between might feel painful, but doggie-paddling while gasping for air and trying to keep afloat hurts more.

When was the last time you created space to dream? When did you last ask yourself—or have you ever?—"What do I *really* want?" You know, that million-dollar question: *If I couldn't fail, what would I do?* Or, if that doesn't do it for you: *If money wasn't a consideration, what would I do?* Forget the sky; that's just the beginning of space. *You* set the limit.

I've coached many clients on this. So far, in 100 percent of cases, the big dream is not a trip to the moon. It is attainable. But you have to see and feel it first. Feel its edges, see its shape, and imagine you're there—until suddenly, you are.

That's the paradox: You don't dare to dream because you fear it will be impossible to grasp, but when you stop to imagine what you *really* want, you discover it's within reach. Sure, you have to grow into it—otherwise, you're not dreaming big enough—but it is possible and plausible. But you need to stop, pause, reflect, and give yourself space.

Coaching certification made me stop in my tracks and ask questions, like what I really wanted. The last time I asked myself what I wanted was for Chrismukkah, but definitely not in life. I didn't think I could. Strange, isn't it? The *shift* starts not with the answer but with asking the right question.

Luckily, you have the answer. It's in there, rising up when it can, bubbling to the surface when given a bit of air. It's in the thoughts flashing on the ceiling before you fall asleep, keeping you awake. It's in the thing you're avoiding. I had the answer too. I wanted to design my own days. Despite the peaks and the valleys, I wouldn't change launching Kollektiv Studio for anything. *I have never felt more alive.* And my dreams keep getting bigger as I expand to meet them.

Dreaming is the beginning of limitless possibilities. It's the wild beyond within. Let the dream be hazy and fuzzy but deeply felt. It's not meant to be judged, realistic, or a plan. It's a walk in the woods, a nonsensical daydream, a road trip to a truck stop diner for pie, asking yourself which slice you *really* want.

Fieldwork

Create space and time, play your favorite music, get comfortable, and bring a pen and paper to sketch your dream future or creative venture.

Give yourself permission to be completely unreasonable and unrealistic. *What's your dream? What's your moonshot?*

Structure unstructured time in your calendar. Give your mind space to wander. Rediscover play. Give yourself a dose of that never-ending summer vacation feeling. *What does unstructured time look like to you?*

Craft multiple futures. Dreams can easily be seen as plans. So, we're going to trick the mind by creating multiple dreams and futures. With multiple possible realities, you don't have to reach or achieve any of them. They're just playful ideas and wild imaginings.

Remember: You can create whatever future you want.

- Create multiple future scenarios—at least three.
- What do these futures *feel* like?

Review your futures: Which one would you most like to inhabit? Why?

where it lives
a poem for creative seekers

the remnant of a dream
caked in the corner of eyes
creased pillows and rumpled hair
stumbling for a steaming cup of joe
the shape of what could be created
lost in the morning rush.

the arteries of ideas clog,
hardened by
too many *kind regards*
doom-scrolling
reading lines from
other people's stories
instead of making our own.

creativity folded and packed
as we travel to somewhere
distracted by the promise of
what's at the end of the rainbow,
we forget to see its colors
before it disappears.

creativity marinates
when lost in thought
ideas bubble like marinara sauce
the sound of cicadas
interrupting daydreams,
releasing a memory with a basil top note,
from a summer that feels never-ending.

now is later (eat the avocado)

I opened the orange and white shoebox and smelled plastic, cardboard, and leather. I'm fourteen and worked all summer at Moishe's Diner to save for this pair of Nikes. The air conditioner rattled and the bell rang every time a customer came in or out, making me and Norma sweat.

We worked the counter next to the kitchen, fried onions, french fry oil, and wafting heat creating a can't-wait-to-clock-out vibe. I served egg creams—an eggless blend of iced milk, seltzer and flavored syrup; Diet Cokes and slices of chocolate cake, a duo that confused me; and refilled countless cups of coffee.

I had a crush on Antonio, a beautiful, colorful, kind, and—though I didn't realize it—gay Puerto Rican waiter who loved listening to the pop hits on KISS FM. I preferred The Cure's "Lullaby" to his "I Wonder If I Take You Home." Access to Antonio, dill pickles, and everything bagels with cream cheese and lox made up for customers short on time and patience.

I saved my tips in a jar next to my old Cabbage Patch Kid doll in my carpet-to-ceiling pink bedroom until summer ended and I could afford to buy my coveted Nikes, a pair of sneakers I ended up not wearing. Instead, I frequently opened the box to gaze at the perfect, not smudged or scuffed, sneakers.

My father caught me peeking at the shoes and laughed. "Why don't you wear them? You waited all summer to buy them just to keep them in a box?"

I looked down at the pink carpet. "I don't want to get them dirty. I want to save them for a bit."

Most of the time, saving lasted for more than "a bit." I never really thought twice about it. I kept my shoes in boxes for months before wearing them. Even as an adult, when I do buy nice things, I hesitate to use them, waiting to light that new smoky leather-scented candle, keeping my new notepad crisp and white, and not wearing that new shirt *yet*—behavior I never questioned, until now.

Fast-forward thirty years later: I'm in the kitchen, contemplating whether I should eat a perfectly ripe avocado. I think, *Maybe I should save it*. I am aware of the thought. Why would I save a ready-to-eat avocado? It will spoil later, so what gives? Where does this idea come from? I take the question to my therapist, Christina.

"I almost stopped myself from eating a perfectly ripe avocado today," I tell Christina. "I thought that I should save it for later, which is so weird. And it's not just avocados, it's new boots and money and tons of other stuff. Where does this come from?"

"Well, as a child, you had to save your reserves for what might be coming next to protect yourself. And chaos usually did come. So you didn't allow yourself to enjoy and relax in the moment you were in."

I take a sip of the lukewarm instant coffee with not enough Coffee-Mate, forcing myself to swallow. "So I didn't let myself enjoy the moment because I was afraid of leaving myself exposed to whatever might come next?"

"It served you as a child. It helped you survive. The question is: Is it still useful?"

"No. It stops me from fully enjoying my life. Holding back and saving means I am forfeiting joy now."

"Protecting yourself created a distrust in life."

Sunlight forming golden zebra stripes on the wall behind Christina's plush chair distracts me from the rush of emotion.

"You didn't allow yourself to relax into the moment and enjoy what's available to you, whether Nikes or an avocado, because you were afraid it would leave you defenseless to what might be coming down the road."

I fiddle with the striped pillows and sit a bit straighter. "That feels sad. I stopped myself from enjoying life now to protect myself from an uncertain future."

"But today, when you picked up the avocado, you were aware of the thought. That's change; that's choice. You've been working your way here."

That therapy session left me in a fog of grief, my legs like lead. I robbed myself of joy because I was scared of being vulnerable and unprepared when shit happened in the future. The veins in my temple throb. I'm going straight home to put on my never-worn cashmere sweater, order expensive sushi, and enjoy every raw bite wrapped in goat fur.

New life goal—pleasure now. Enjoying this lush and ludicrous life in the skin I'm in on this strange rock. I am going to enjoy the hell out of *whatever* life serves me, like Oysters Rockefeller and Gruyère and Crab Palmiers at a Hollywood producer's party. *Yes, please. Thank you. I'll have another one.* I'll be wearing a YSL long silk black dress, channeling Michelle Pfeiffer in *Scarface*, reaching for a glass of bubbly on silver trays with a look of wild glee in my eyes. It might take time to arrive at this black tie affair, but I'll be working my way to it, one avocado at a time.

Going into the belly of the belief beast

I interviewed Christina, curious about how we rewrite old scripts, create new realities and experiences, and change our behavior.

"When we change habits, we need two things: to make a decision and have courage. Because if you want to change it, if you want to go into your own pleasure, then you need to make the decision, *This is what I want*, and then have the emotional courage to do it."

"What requires courage?" I asked.

"It takes courage to loosen and liberate yourself from the shame, guilt, anxiety—everything connected to the old core belief, and say, *I can eat this, I can enjoy it. And it's okay.* You need the courage to stop what stopped you. Therapy is about being in a new process in a relevant adult age, bringing the child into the process, and saying, 'We're going to try again,' and work to identify, understand, then change. It's all about rewriting the story and seeing opportunities that were there but not available for you to understand. Suddenly you started thinking, *Yes, why don't I enjoy my avocado? Why can I not enjoy it?* You start mentally working with the thought of what you want it to be."

Working with the thought of what you want it to be creates new neural pathways.

"[Your brain] is constantly changing," says Louise Hansen, a psychologist in Edmonton, Australia. "You can participate in that process. This means things are not permanent as we once thought they were and also that you can heal trauma."[1]

Once seen as a static organ, the brain constantly changes based on experience. Neuroplasticity is the brain's remarkable capacity to reorganize itself by forming new neural connections and modifying existing ones.[2]

We can break free from old patterns by repeating new activities and behaviors. The more we practice, the stronger the neural pathways grow, making the new behavior feel more routine and natural over time.

It takes roughly ten thousand repetitions, or around three months of consistent practice, to solidify a new neural pathway and master a new behavior pattern.[3]

Synaptic pruning is what the brain does when new neural pathways are strengthened through learning and new experiences and less frequently used neural pathways become weak and eventually die (*stab, stab*).[4] This requires consistency, practice, and commitment. When you develop a new habit, the old one becomes a choice—an option that you can choose to live without.

Now I get to choose. I can rewrite the belief and know I can trust life and myself to creatively respond to whatever comes my way. This frees me to fully enjoy the moment I'm in; to eat the avocado, wear the white Nikes, and spend the money, not save it for rainy days but use it to create sunny ones. It's a practice, like so many things in this book.

There are no easy formulas or get-healed-quick schemes. Every time I catch myself holding back from enjoying something *now*, I realign and open to joy, savoring whatever life is serving me.

The real strengthening of any new muscle happens in the small, sometimes seemingly inconsequential daily life moments. At dinner the other night, I considered *not* using a napkin because I thought I should save the nice ones for guests, using a paper towel instead. I caught it and then rebelliously pulled the angelic white napkin out of the gold palm leaf holder, and dabbed the spaghetti sauce on the side of my mouth like a queen. It is easier to strengthen new habits in a myriad of small ways than wait for the *big* challenge that triggers an automatic reaction because you haven't been working the weaker muscles out.

Living a creative life requires becoming aware of who authored the core belief—the child or the adult?—and choosing accordingly. Most importantly, it needs you to be here, present to all that is unfolding right now, in this moment. Not deferring happiness to protect yourself from pain, chaos, and disappointment, which will happen whether you brace for impact or not; whether you rob yourself of joy now or not; whether you make some secret deal with the universe under your pillow fort—*some of my happiness for your protection*—or not.

It's feeling it all or removing the blocks to feeling. It's rewriting scripts that lead you to repeat tired, old behaviors that keep you in the same party at different venues. You deserve more than chips and crackers with Cheez Whiz. Creatively directing your experience requires examining your relationship with life and deciding which pathways to strengthen and fade. I don't know about you, but I'll be eating ripe avocados in my fresh Air Jordans.

Fireside chat

It's easy to forget the quality, texture, and flavor you want your days to have. The big goal gets all the attention and focus, but not how it will *feel* when you get there, when you inhabit it. Your days might be spent moving in a way that's the opposite of how you want to live, hoping that when you get "there"—that beautiful utopian hazy oasis—you'll experience flow, ease, and fulfillment.

So you defer happiness today, hoping it will all make sense, the pieces will fit together, and you'll elegantly slip into the desired future like a silk kimono as you rise from your deck chair overlooking the ocean in Capri. Here's the raw deal: If you don't create it now, you won't get it later. No amount of pushing, driving, and squeezing the air out of your days will get you to the promised land. All that does is move you *away* from it.

Think about it: You're rushing, hoping it will get you to a slower place and pace. The more you reinforce this behavior daily, the deeper its groove and pattern.

Unfortunately, as you may have guessed, the answer is not a simple, instantaneous one. You need to start cultivating the way you want to move and be *now*. You might say, "But, Pia, how can I live as though I have what I don't have?" And I'd reply, "What you're really after is a *feeling* of having, not the actual possession of the object."

Remember the orgasmic feeling of unboxing a new pair of Air Max? It passes *quickly*. More than material goods, you're hungry for a feeling—a feeling of safety, freedom, satisfaction, enoughness, validation. Pick your pleasure. We like quick fixes, easy outs, so the object, however fleeting, is easier to obtain than the search for what fuels it. And definitely easier than designing our experience of life, right here, right now. Easy? No. Worthwhile? A screaming full-body yes.

So how do you create the feeling? Remind yourself of what brings you that feeling *now*. Start embodying the most you version of yourself and how you want life to be *now*. If it's a feeling of freedom you're after, and you think that the next big paycheck or payout will get you there, ask yourself: *What makes me feel free now?* Start doing those things daily. If safety is on the other side of that raise or sale, ask yourself: *What makes me feel safe?* Do these practices every day. We often avoid doing the hard work of imagining what we want and desire and bringing that to life in the here and now.

It's not a destination; it's a daily practice. Get curious about what blocks this feeling and how you want to invite it into the expanse of your days. When I ask my clients what brings them joy, no one—not one—mentions material goods. They list what they have right now: the intangible mundane and magical details of this life; the touch of a hand, sunlight on the skin, grass in between toes, a deep conversation.

Don't get sucked into the idea that once you acquire something, that feeling you're chasing will not only appear but will *remain*. It will head out before you wake up, leaving you with lipstick-stained wine glasses and underwear crumpled on the floor.

Stop waiting and hoping that feeling of safety, security, happiness, satisfaction, and fulfillment is somewhere out there, in the yonder, almost within grasp, and that next purchase, raise, or goal will take you there. **That's the biggest lie out there.** If you don't create it now, you won't have it later. I'm saying it again for the people in the back— and for myself.

Fieldwork

The Joy List. *What brings you joy?* Grab a stack of Post-its. Set a timer to two minutes. Write *one* idea per Post-it. Go for quantity over quality. Choose two to ten things from your list and do them this week. Observe the impact.

Now do the exercise with a friend, family member, or partner. Afterward, share your lists. What's the impact of sharing and hearing each other's joy givers? How do you feel afterward?

A day in your life. Imagine you can design a day in your future—let's say a year from now—down to the detail, however you'd like. You're the designer. What would your perfect day look like? Describe every detail—from the moment you wake up to when your head hits the pillow, going through each of the things you'd love to experience.

Create it now: What elements from this day could you bring into your daily life?

Reflect on the feeling: Throughout this gorgeous day in your life, what feeling are you chasing—freedom, happiness, or safety? What will create that feeling *now*? As in, today?

Feeling stumped? Write down what you love to experience. How does doing these things make you feel? How might you integrate these moments in your life now?

pleasure principle
a love poem for the universe

Bring all of me online. All systems go. Nothing held back. *L'Chaim.*

Leaning against a truck in Joshua Tree, local coffee in hand, laughing at being lost in the desert, Lana Del Ray on the radio. Picking a designer dress off the rack when not on sale because I've pried fear's grip, finger by finger, from my wrist. Being seen because I reveal who I am and (the pleasure of) our entrainment, frequencies swaying, scribbling our initials, an arrow through a heart. Savoring each mussel swimming in white wine sauce (dropping history) to the laughter of my mother. Setting down heavy bags, hair plastered to my forehead, changing into a bikini and charging into the pool, chlorine splashing sunbathers.

Rolling with life, car window down, elbow on the edge, breeze raising goosebumps, toes smudging the windshield, chest full, nothing but watermelon Lip Smackers, shades, and a phone loaded with joint playlists, riding into the Valley of the Gods like I'm landing on Mars. Releasing ideas of where my love needs to live, no longer safe in an apartment in Park Slope, but like a smoke machine, it has no domicile, it slips under doors and makes every place a party. Breaking my heart to open, pieces flying everywhere, only to get caught in our teeth like popcorn kernels at movies we fall in love with. Sunburned and freckled, hair sprayed with Sun In, skin dosed in Coke and baby oil before we knew better, braided hair, the discovery of orgasms.

Fucking pleasure. It's everywhere. In the sun's kiss, the heart of an artichoke, art that makes me cry, chopped onions and heartache. In the monstera plant that shows me how to take up space, in the Billie Eilish track that turns my kitchen into a dance floor. In the sleep caught in the edges of your eyes, hair trying to escape your scalp, walking toward me with a half smile, sleepy. In our deep thundering kiss, tongues lightening, bringing on the storm. In the sweat gathering under my breasts and the small of my back as I shake and spin. In the white suede candle flickering on a day when the rain hits windows, your fingers tracing the ridges of my backbone, reading my spine like braille. In the moon, a pin, reminding me where I am, beyond earthly routines. In the breeze carrying gardenia and leaving a bouquet at my feet.

Pleasure, it's everywhere. Waiting for you to pull it in like a dying lover, with an urgency that makes the universe hold its breath, on the edge of its seat, consumed by the scenes you're creating.

champagne problems

My mom white knuckles the wheel of her brown beat-up Chevrolet truck. I'm visiting her in Hamilton, Ontario. A hefty incentive lured her from Montreal to this sprawling port city in dire need of speech pathologists. This means she has to drive, which she learned late in life, and her yellow-stained fingers shake at the wheel. The dream catcher, with its leather web and fuchsia feathers, swings on the front view mirror, the smell of cigarettes stale in the air.

I'm twenty-three years old, muttering about driving through this freezing industrial wasteland, my breath coming out in smoke, as we make our way to buy wine for a dinner party with her friends. We pull up in front of the Liquor Control Board of Ontario (LCBO), the government-controlled dispensary, ice cracking as the tires drive into the parking spot. We open the heavy doors, wind rushes us in, and my mom makes her way to the French section and chooses two bottles of the cheapest *vin de table*.

"Mom, do we really need two bottles?"

My mother looks at me like I'm the most exasperating daughter alive. "Of course we do," she replies. "We are going to be five people, because Lenka's son might come, and we'll be eating dinner. Don't police me."

I stomp down the Australian aisle, the dark shiraz and berry pinots winking at me, and head toward the exit.

My mother, wearing her favorite color red leather red boots, blue jeans, and an Eddie Bauer sweater she bought at Winners, Canada's favorite discount store, waves goodbye to the cashier, hands me the clinking black plastic bag, and says, "Prend ça et met le dans la coffre" (*take this and put it in the trunk*), as she pulls out a du Maurier and fights to light it in the dusting snow.

We return to my mom's flat with its uncomfortable futon covered by an itchy striped Peruvian blanket, my father's abstract art on the walls, piles of *New Yorker* magazines, and ashtrays and start to prepare for the evening. My mom makes a simple quiche Lorraine as an appetizer, drinking white wine with ice cubes as she cooks and sings Tracy Chapman's "Fast Car." I chop parsley, feeling uneasy about the early start on the wine, until it is time to go. Luckily, given the -6°F weather, we only have to go upstairs to Jerry and Lenka's.

Later that evening, after mashed potatoes, roast chicken, and at least four bottles of wine, Jerry pulls out the drums, and Lenka and I start to dance, both moving unsteadily, feet absorbed by the carpet, bodies slackened by alcohol, as my mom sits and rolls a joint with fingers decorated with turquoise. I'm closer to my mother in the sway of alcohol. I wake up with regret on my tongue and a sinking feeling. Something's lost in the space between last night and the morning after.

This was one of many parties.

As a child, I poured my mom's wine bottles down the sink and hid her cigarettes. I hated the sour and acidic smell of wine; how it slurred my mother's speech, lowered her eyelids, slowed her movements. I never knew who would come out to play. I pinky-promised myself I would never drink or smoke, and I held out for a long time, until I fell underneath it and allowed what I had been fighting for so long to wash over me. Wine became our connective tissue, either my rebellion against it or my eventual acquiescence to it. I get caught in its tannin-y clutches.

At seventeen, I get kicked out after my mother comes home drunk—again—and wants to talk. I had a terrible day at school, which means I was in the principal's office for something, and I just wanted to sleep. My mother won't leave me alone, so I snap and lock her outside our apartment door. I just want it to stop. I need to be left alone. The door to my own bedroom doesn't lock, but the front door does. When I hear the click, air pushes out of my lungs in a deep sigh. I go right to bed.

My aunt lives downstairs, and she has a key to our apartment. After a few glorious minutes of silence, my aunt and mom burst through the door.

"You can't do this to your mother," my aunt screeches. She grabs handfuls of my clothes and tosses them down the apartment stairwell.

Oh shit. I'm getting kicked out. Watching my cargo pants and striped tube top fly in the air above me feels surreal, as if I'm watching this happening to someone else. My mind empty, nervous laughter almost erupting, body frozen in place, just blankly staring at two sisters throwing my clothes like snowballs.

My mother chimes in. "Come back when you learn to live by *my* rules."

As a child who parented herself, I'm livid that I'm expected to now listen to her. I'm also dead tired of the drinking and our hyperstrained relationship, so I leave. I never live with my mother, or a parent, again.

Thirty years later, I'm in the kitchen of my mom's casita in Mexico, the screen door open, and the sound of birds and yelps of neighborhood dogs mix with Lila Downs singing loudly, the teal iPhone holder and amplifier she made in her ceramics class working wonders. She drops an octopus leg with a splash in the boiling water, laurel leaves swimming to the surface. She pauses, tucks a strand of her platinum bob behind her ear, takes a drag of her cigarette, looks at me pensively, and says, "It's a good thing you don't have kids so you can focus on your creativity."

I try not to let that one bruise me, but it does anyway. It jabs with a left, landing on an infertility wound, and with a right, on the child who blames herself for her mother's inability to create. The sting didn't last long because it wasn't raising a kid that killed my mom's creativity, though surely survival and caring for me played a part. Addiction was the main culprit. Alcohol is a cotton ball that absorbs time and creativity.

For my mom, the daughter of a warm and eccentric alcoholic father and a bona fide hippie, alcohol is the solution. It is what punctuates days. After a long day at work, the reward is a glass—never just one—of wine. Deeper conversations brought to you by alcohol. A party is not a party without wine and cigarettes. Need to sleep? Take a sip and a toke. Alcohol is a friend, a shoulder to lean on, a salve, a cure, a party favor, a ticket out of here, but never a creativity enabler.

So let's kick another creative myth off the cultural shelf: Alcohol and drugs fuel creativity. They don't. They force you to abandon it, to choose another over it, to relegate creativity to mistress status, and she does not flourish as a part-time lover. She shrivels from disregard, from being tended to momentarily and gruffly, with the fuzzy peach of a hangover. Yet, the false link between alcohol and creativity has remained embedded in our cultural consciousness.

A psychological study conducted by the University of Essex and Humboldt University of Berlin found that drugs do not enhance creativity. In fact, narcotics were identified as the least effective means to inspire imagination. Their subsequent paper showed that while people on psilocybin, a favorite in Silicon Valley for sparking creativity, felt more creative, they actually performed worse than when they were sober.[1]

"I thought that the drinking and the drug use were enabling my creativity," says Julia Cameron, author of *The Artist's Way*, which has sold more than four million copies. "We have a mythology that tells us artists should be drunk and in pain." Before writing the book, Cameron was addicted to alcohol and cocaine. After a nervous breakdown when her marriage with Martin Scorsese crumbled, she got sober. That's when she wrote the best-selling practical guide to "creativity as a spiritual practice"—when clean.[2]

In his study, psychiatrist Dr. Iain Smith found that many famous artists and writers who were known for substance abuse actually created their best work while sober. Smith, an addiction expert from Gartnavel Royal Hospital in Glasgow, argued that alcohol and drugs often stifled creativity rather than enhance it.[3] The idea that substance use fuels the creative process is a dangerous myth.[4] "The reason why this myth is so powerful is the allure of the substances and the fact that many artists need drugs to cope with their emotions. Artists are, in general, more emotional people."[5] Amy Winehouse's deep sensitivity to pain meant she made music that resonated with the world. Unfortunately, that same sensitivity led her to try to dull the pain with alcohol and drugs.[6] Alcohol and drugs do not fuel creativity; they numb sensitivity.

Nancy C. Andreasen, a leading neuroscientist who spent decades studying creativity, says that creatives have to confront doubt and rejection. "And yet they have to persist in spite of that, because they believe strongly in the value of what they do. This can lead to psychic pain, which may manifest itself as depression or anxiety, or lead people to attempt to reduce their discomfort by turning to pain relievers such as alcohol."[7]

As creatives, we're not doomed to fall down the addiction hole. We can feel deeply, create from this place, and thrive and connect. Once we're aware of the support we need, we can give it to ourselves. Researchers stressed there's no one-size-fits-all for cultivating creativity; people respond differently to various methods and situations. A comprehensive review of hundreds of studies found that complex training courses, meditation, and cultural exposure, like studying abroad, are the most effective ways to boost creativity. And it's clear: Alcohol and drugs don't make the list.[8]

Art requires honesty. It needs us to show up to the page, the canvas, the mold, and not only fully inhabit life but be deeply present for it, which is the opposite of what alcohol and drugs beckon us to do. They're the easy escape hatch—a fast track to feeling good, but then it fades. Life becomes torn, like a French baguette ripped by hungry hands, into two pieces: the duty-filled world of sobriety versus the enticing world of rocket highs, wobbly dances, fits of laughter, and bouts of complete and total forgetfulness. The days drag on, fingers drumming on tables, waiting to clutch a glass of vino.

My mother splits into two to inhabit these worlds. In the gray, she can be tough, sharp, directive; in the multihued, she is warm, funny, vivacious, lit up, yet sometimes mean and short-tempered, depending on the mood and the drug of choice.

I witnessed this as a kid and I experienced it as an adult, unconsciously following similar patterns. It's 2004, and I'm an undergrad student at Hunter College on the upper west side in New York City, majoring in the interdisciplinary field of writing, art, and literature. I chose Hunter because one of my heroes, Audre Lorde, a feminist and activist poet extraordinaire, attended and taught in the English department until 1986.

I heard many renowned teachers from Columbia and NYU also taught at Hunter to give back, so that, along with the incentive of not graduating saddled with debt, sealed my choice. I threw myself into studying, writing a paper on the *Three Graces*, a neoclassical sculpture in marble of Zeus's daughters that I stared at for an hour at the MET for my art history class.

The teacher accuses me of plagiarism because the paper is so good I couldn't have possibly written it. I defend my honor and my case until the teacher capitulates and apologizes. I squeeze tightly into the six train during rush hour, clutching my books to my chest, until the car empties after the Fifty-ninth Street Bridge.

I work as a bartender at a bar on the Lower West Side in Manhattan called Naked Lunch, after William S. Burroughs's book, on Thursday, Friday, and Saturday nights. On a good night, I take home $300 in tips. It's frequented by a strange mix: ad agency people and the occasional European who tips terribly during happy hour; and once the DJ arrives, traders, bridge and tunnel people, and yuppies. The DJ plays hits from the eighties and nineties, and I would happily never listen to "Smooth Criminal" or the "Love Shack" ever again.

My regular customer, a reedy, long-faced young blond man in a suit, probably a Wall Street broker of sorts, walks to the bar and orders his usual, a Glenfiddich and Coke, which makes me shake my internal head. Why would anyone want to dilute a quality whiskey unless to show he has so much money he doesn't care? Either way, I don't care. He tips well and drinks heavily.

As the night wears on, a heavily intoxicated man in a sweat-stained T-shirt comes to the bar and attempts to order a drink— "Cannaigetajackencookee?"—that is so garbled I can barely make it out. And even though I do, I don't serve him a Jack and Coke, replying, "I got one rule: If you can't pronounce the drink, I can't serve it," which is a good rule because in the state of New York, you are liable as a bartender if you serve someone who is clearly incapacitated, and this guy fits the bill beautifully.

I stare out into the sardined crowd swaying to Santana's "Maria Maria," spot a guy intensely rubbing the burgundy velvet curtains while sipping on orange juice, clearly on Molly, and wonder what aliens would think of humans looking at this scene. I am snapped out of my thoughts when I see a friend who bartends at Balthazar, a French bistro, walk up to the corner of the bar. "Hey, Frankie. What's up? What can I get you?" Having two bartenders working an insanely busy Saturday night doesn't leave much room for conversation.

"A margarita, love. Thanks." My pour is always heavy for fellow "staff" and friends. I hand him the glass glowing with sunny tequila.

I deal with drunk people most nights, managing, directing, setting boundaries, and serving them. It's enough to make me never want to touch alcohol again, as a feeling of disgust coats my tongue for most of the night. Until last call, when a switch flips, and all we want to do is have a stiff drink to wash the night away, to unwind, release, have fun. It's our turn now—4:30 a.m. is the witching hour for bartenders and other staff, from barbacks to waiters, getting off their shifts.

Tonight, we head to an Italian restaurant clandestinely open only for people in the business on the corner of West Broadway. The bouncer recognizes us. We move past the heavy curtains, find a candle-lit table in the corner, and order vodka tonics while the sounds of Euro electronica join the smoke circulating around the room. The drinks are strong, the company gets better with each one, and we ignore the sun's rise until it's time to leave or find the next party. Luckily, I usually head home because I will rinse and repeat this the next day.

Until Monday rolls around, and the responsible, dutiful, dedicated student who is adamant about making something of her life gives her studies everything she has got and then lets off all the steam from that pressure cooker when the weekend rolls around. Moving through different extremes and worlds becomes habitual. I shift between the tight disciplinarian who keeps me in line as a *magna cum laude* student at Hunter, and the last-one-standing party girl in the evenings after work.

I write papers and poems and read, but the nights and alcohol, sometimes drugs, absorb any real time required for my creativity to thrive. It's hard to write with a hangover, difficult to feel myself when my brain is soaking in peach flavored Stolichnaya, and challenging to connect dots or ideas when my tongue is cardboard and my memory a dust bunny.

The good girl, bad girl pattern continues with varying intensity, depending on my circumstances. Over the years, I swing from order to chaos and back again. As a commercial creative, my ideas flow into my day job, while at night, I'm either in love, tangled in a sticky relationship, or at a party—until I grow tired of running, extremes, and shape-shifting. This fatigue coincides with the slow walk home to myself, where I choose experiences and habits that bring me closer to myself, not further away.

I stopped drinking in 2020, which also happens to be when my creativity flourished.

It no longer has to compete with escapism and false ecstasy.

After years of drinking while he wrote, best-selling author David Sedaris quit in 1999, challenging the idea that he couldn't create unless he had a drink in his hand. In an NPR interview, he said, "I kind of got it in my head that I needed to be drinking while I wrote... I don't know why I was so convinced of it. It's like saying, 'I can't sing unless I have a blue shirt on.'" The sheer volume of his work in the years that followed proves one thing: It was never the drinking that fueled his sharp, witty genius.[9]

The real link to creativity is sobriety.

But it's not the only one.

thirsty
a poem for the insatiable

the alarm rings *again*,
my chest tightens
(i'm late)
cold water hits my skin
shower curtain sticking to legs
mascara applied to lashes and lids
(what to wear?)
choose something fast
scoff toast, chug instant coffee
air kiss my partner on the way out
to meetings and emails
(hope this finds you well)
commute home
(hurry up, will you?)
return to dinner with one (just one) glass of wine
a show (whatever you want to watch, babe)
fuck (maybe?)
pop two melatonin gummies
sleep (maybe?)
rinse and repeat in slight variations
until Friday,
when aperol spritz,
oaky chardonnay, crisp IPA,
gin and tonic, ruby pinot,
or a bourbon sour with egg whites

       —break the monotony.

blood fizzy, cheeks flaming, eyes glassy
we toss layers of self like peanut shells
revealing nutty centers.
things like used to matter
(decorum, niceties, manners, fidelity)
float like cigarettes in piss-colored beer.

the world stops squatting on my shoulders
i'm so light, the room spins
dust looks like stars in the smoky haze
i'm not solid, I'm 70 percent water and wine
we pee together in the bathroom,
when i stand up, she leans in to kiss me,
cherry print underwear still around my knees,
her sangria lipstick coloring
outside my lines.

our giggles echo
in the graffitied (mary poopins) stall
the steel door slams open
our smudged lips stumble
to the mahogany bar,
two lemon drops to keep euphoria afloat, please.
relegating reality to the shore (you, stay there).
lick, shoot, slam.

time lost, hours chugged, mascara smudged
moments that stitched us together
unravel in the morning sun.
we pick shattered illusions
out of our teeth
and get cut by sharp daylight
as we head home.

i tiptoe into the bathroom
brush the film from my white tongue
slowly peel the sheet back
quietly, softly (please don't wake up)

waking up to cold stares
(did you have fun last night?)
the clatter of plates put in the dishwasher
way too early
head throbbing and wooly
tongue thick in my mouth
keeps words gated
afraid of what might come out.

fuzzy recollections
a phone number on a matchbook
the start of a bruise
(fuck, i hope i didn't do anything stupid)
texting friends for clues
their silence pointed fingers
i wrap myself in the comforter
hoping to disappear into vampires on screen
that pull me away from anxious thoughts
sticking to my lungs like tar.

guilt floods in with the relentless sun
(why can't it rain?)
knots my stomach like a skilled sailor
twist, bend, tuck, pull, tighten
burns like that game we played as kids
snake bite
shame setting my skin on fire
regret playing my body
like sweaty Mozart at the piano

until one day,
i wake up tired of being tired
tired of forgetting, losing, bruising, running.
done with the insatiable hunger for more
done tearing apart what I build
with famished hands
ripping it apart like a baguette.
my waking life in tatters on the floor
between black lace bras and blackouts,
overflowing ashtrays and crushing shame.

i discover the escape hatch is a trap
a jail cell disguised as wilderness
that can become a life sentence
if i keep locking myself in,
and throwing vodka the keys.
i brake hard and
                stop.

no longer waiting to get off
the merry-go-round of adulting,
i stay on the horse and gallop.
wind gently blowing
the hair out of my eyes,
so i can see
so i can feel
and be present for
and with everything.
knowing this, right here,
is a ride I want to stay on.

i want to lock lips with experience
get licked, loved, spanked,
brought to my knees
and whisked away by reality
on the dance floor like a girl at prom.
(forever young)

i want real intimacy,
his hand on my knee
legs intertwined
as we read books together
while the "Sunset in Capri" candle
burns and Miles Davis shows
us another kind of blue
in a stillness that caresses
my nervous system.

i want to eat an artichoke
slowly, intentionally,
bathe steamed purple and green
leaves in dijon vinaigrette
pluck, dip, pull
(sliding its flesh down my teeth).

i want to feel sweat
gathering under my bra
when I sway my hips, arms in the air,
and belt out the wrong lyrics to a song
with my feet firmly planted on the floor.

i want to wake up guilt-free
eat a bowl of crispy courage to:
create the art that is my life
not abandon myself,
break generational trauma,
choose to heal instead of hide.

i want to feel it all
get high on the endless supply
of everything
right here,
right now,
when i am present
                    for it.

you're the secret sauce

I'm a shapeshifter. Not of the X-Men variety, unfortunately. I've been changing shapes since 1975, and twenty-five years later, it was no different. Friday night in Manhattan stretches ahead, glimmering like an iridescent pearl, and I'm ready to shuck the oyster to find it.

Angie, one of my closest friends and a fellow shapeshifter, and I hail a yellow cab and ride into the meat-packing district. Our legs and patent heels spill out of the taxi and into the lobby of a sleek high-rise hotel. As the elevator climbs to the rooftop terrace, I gaze at Angie, her dark wavy hair framing a heart-shaped baby face, lips glossed and greased, red dress hugging her hips, metallic booties elevating her to my height.

In this 360-degree mirrored box, I barely see traces of the girl with a sloppy bun, a Guns N' Roses T-shirt and sweats, and visible freckles who sat on my couch an hour ago. The door pings open to a rooftop scene from *Wolf of Wall Street*—if it were made then—and we walk out, shoulders back, heads held high, like debutantes entering society.

Traders in suspenders, white shirts, and exposed chest hair talk in packs. Our bodies flow and thrum through the suited crowd, stopping for a free espresso martini and the obligatory small talk, feeling the adrenaline and the burn in our throats as we collect business cards we'll use to blot our lips later. Walking to the roof's edge, I lean against the railing, silk black dress fluttering in the wind, goosebumps on my skin, and stare into the pupils of the city's dazzling lights, neon signs, and mismatched buildings.

Tired of stiff bodies, we find another taxi and head to Alphabet City. We're in search of a nondescript black door, the entrance to an underground party a friend texted us about. We knock, the door creaks open, steam greets us, and we slink in. The room roars with the bass of tribal house. It beats in us, each pulse increasing our heart rates.

Everyone is dressed in black, covered in tattoos and piercings, shaking their bodies in a trance. We dance, cells rearranging. The walls sweat, and our skin glistens as we sway on the sticky floor amid Dominicans in feathered fedoras and black eyeliner. After the shine fades, we head out to a lounge on the Lower West Side. The wind sends a chill down our spines, and we're buzzing with possibility.

We enter Life, its neon script popping against the dark blue sky. A DJ spins, a drag queen stomps to the hard beat of "Do It Again," and models and musicians drape over leather couches, some with iced nostrils. We're possessed by the spirit of Kate Moss, lithe and slim, untouchable, almost floating through the crowded bottle tables. A music producer in his thirties with a solid mullet, gold chain, Hawaiian shirt exposing chest hair, and leather pants offers us a seat at his table, where a bottle of Dom glows in the limelight. We slide into the booth, laughing with our mouths wide open, as we spill champagne after slamming our glasses together. Again, we're right at home.

Moving through crowds and cultures feels like unmoored freedom. We lose ourselves in the night in shapes, accents, music, dance floor oases, and secret and obnoxious buildings. It's a buffet with no theme, egg foo young served with chicken waffles.

The problem with being a shapeshifter is this: If you keep changing shapes, you forget your original form and have trouble shifting back into it. How do you return to your design when you've worn so many outfits, from capes to three-piece suits, some of them even still draped over you? How do you recognize the skin you're in?

We can all change shapes based on our surroundings, upbringing, and culture. It is one of the skills that enables us to survive and succeed in society. We're reared to fill and follow a certain form, usually based on the ideals of those in power: generally white, heterosexual, able, extroverted, and assertive men.

Life itself also has a recognizable, acceptable mold and sequence to follow: Get an education, graduate from college (usually in debt); find a reputable job (preferably in business, law, or medicine), earn a good, solid living; meet your partner, get married, have kids, save for a 401K, retire, and then enjoy the fruit of all your labor. The promise of the American dream uttered with a white-toothed Colgate smile. Thank God for New York City, the home of weirdos, rebels, artists, and the Yankees.

What happens when you come from two vastly different cultures, raised across cities and countries? How do you recognize yourself? I've been moving between two different homes since my parents separated when I was three. Spanish came more naturally than French, my mother's native tongue, because I went to preschool in Spain. I wasn't Jewish, since my mom is Catholic. I wasn't cut from my mother's blonde, green-eyed cloth, but instead have wavy, big dark hair and brown eyes. I wanted so badly to belong to someone, a group, a place, and spent years trying on outfits to make that happen. But it didn't, because it's never me, not really.

When I got married for the first time in Morocco, I was brought in on a palanquin carried by four men. I was smiling, like a fool, when I was supposed to look sad, because traditionally, this is when the woman leaves her family, all she has known. And I am grinning wildly like the Chesterfield cat. My ex-husband's family asks if I took Arabic dancing lessons before the wedding because they were shocked at how well I danced, as if I were from Casablanca. The truthful answer would be "I'm a shapeshifter. I adapt quickly." Instead, I replied, "No, not really, but I lived in Bahrain." This is true to an extent. I did dance in Manama, but to house music in a club with members of the elite (no one else could afford to risk their reputations), Emirates flight attendants, and other foreigners. My new husband's family smiled approvingly, and the dance continued.

I am wearing pounds of gold in the form of a WWE style belt and jewelry we rented from a wedding coordinator, or *negafa*. Again, I was supposed to sit demurely on the white sofa placed in the middle of the ballroom. The *negafa* anxiously watched over me as I moved under the weight of a jewel-encrusted gold crown. Despite the eyes boring into me, sweat pouring down my neck, tightly bobby-pinned crown, and itch of crinoline and polyester, I shake my weighted hips to the beat of drums, my hands flicking and arms weaving in the air defiantly.

The biggest act of rebellion is to write your own story and live it. Switching outfits on set is exhausting. You need to remember your lines. Feel the room instead of feeling yourself. Develop a sharp, powerful antenna that registers what's expected of you at any moment. Anticipate what people need to keep yourself in character, accepted, and safe.

If people saw me for who I really was, and I did nothing to please them, would I be loved and welcomed? All this shape-shifting erodes the original form and confidence, love, and acceptance of self. It becomes a prison, a corset that makes it hard to breathe. There is nothing more liberating than tearing off a heavy gold belt, crown, and beaded dress, putting on a pair of jeans and a white T-shirt, and dancing to your own inner rhythm under the light and encouragement of the moon. Talk about deep breaths.

  "Be yourself. Everyone else is taken."[1]

—Oscar Wilde

At some point, you need to stop letting the story write you and start writing it.

After almost two years in business, I am working with a creative coach to connect the dots of my brand story. We explore big, annoying—because they require serious digging and looking back—questions, like: *How does creativity and coaching come together in my business? Why me? Why now? What brought me here? What do I take a stand for? What uniquely places me to do the work I do? What's my story?* I am taken through an exercise where I write momentous and character-shaping events that occurred through different seven-year phases of my life since birth, seeing it all through the lens of my business, my brand, and what I uniquely offer the world.

A study examined how creativity has the potential to help us create meaning of our life history.[2] Looking back, we make sense of the past by creating our story and assigning our role within it, which helps us "successfully cope with challenging experiences, such as trauma, regret, or nostalgia."[3] Research demonstrates that writing about past experiences builds a sense of coherence and well-being. Both literary scholars and cognitive neuropsychologists agree that constructing narratives is how humans make sense of their experiences and process conflict.

Writing about life experiences creates an "autobiographical gap," a term coined by Rita Charon, pioneer of narrative medicine, to describe the distance between the writer and the actor. Charon states, "Any time a person writes about himself or herself, a space is created between the person doing the writing and the person doing the living, even though, of course, these two people are identical." This space creates a certain distance that enables us to reflect on our own actions, thoughts, or life. Within this reflective space, we discover a heightened way to see ourselves, "revealing fresh knowledge about [our] coherent existence."[4]

I've never been good at looking back. Shape-shifting requires an unyielding focus on the present. It doesn't offer an opportunity to look back and reflect. Looking back is dangerous. I might get lost and stuck in a quicksand of shame and pain. It scares me. This exercise of examining my past is hard. It requires me to gather and fold clothes strewn across many rooms in the mansion of my mind and pack them into a suitcase. I get to pick which pieces, hold them up and inspect them, and then either fold them delicately into my LV suitcase or give them to Goodwill.

> *"Telling our story does not merely document who we are; it helps to make us who we are."*[5]
>
> —Rita Charon

Not every memory needs to be part of the fold. I sigh as I clean, observe, and order my memories, cracking open a guava La Croix, wondering when this will end. It's painful and integrative. I welcome parts of myself home. I am stronger for having the courage to *really* look and bring the lonely, sensitive little girl, the rebellious and endlessly fearless and optimistic teenager, and the many women I've been over the decades together to craft the signature flavor I am meant to infuse into the world today. All the material is here. I just need to witness and gather it with help, in partnership. This is my move into self-authorship and writing my *live* autobiography.

I am able to make sense of my past and see how it brought me here. My unconventional nomadic childhood, separated parents from different cultures, my mother's desire to be free yet oddly tied to her addictions, my father's sensitivity and art, and NYC itself as some strange kind of parent all cultivated my creativity. It developed my ability to imagine, dream, and conceive different realities and stories and connect deeply to others even if just for short periods of time.

I wouldn't change my past for anything. It's made me who I am. All of it—the shit and the sunshine, the bruises and the beauty marks—forged me. I get to rewrite my story, make sense of it, and assign meaning to it. This book is an even bigger exercise in returning to my original form. Rewriting my story not only shapes who I am but who I am becoming. It's my story to tell and live.

When you start to crush hard on who you are today, you honor everything it took to get you here. You welcome all parts of yourself and bring them into the present. I learn how to honor the gifts that came out of chaos: the ability to create colorful worlds and futures when my reality was dim; connect deeply with people, *really* feel them quickly; and the force of action to make things happen. I see how it enables me to bring ideas, art, and businesses into the world, for myself, as a writer, founder, and creative, and for others, as a creative partner and coach.

I deeply understand chaos, change, and creativity. It's my upbringing, it's in my blood, and that makes me a powerful partner for people in relationship with change and creativity—those who desire it, feel its pull, and are in the throes of it. God knows I've built new futures for myself again and again and have lived many different lifetimes in this one life. I've been in the thick goo of transformation; in the dark, the light; up, down, and all around. I have been able to create new worlds for myself, so I know they are not only possible but here, breathing softly, waiting to be inhabited.

After a lifetime of shape-shifting, I rediscovered my original form: that I am forged by fire and air. My bones no longer break, tendons snapping, as I contort myself into new shapes. Instead, I turn my finely tuned antenna inward. I feel myself, the softness of deep breaths, the solid weight of my body, and a heightened self-awareness that changes my experience of the world. I find out that home is wherever I am. I stop trying to belong anywhere, because I have a passport to everywhere.

I learned that inner shifts create real transformation, because once you change, everything changes.

Big talk

Storytelling is an experience of empowerment, a way of honoring your journey and creating from it. It's not only the past you get to reframe and rewrite but your future, and all of it is happening now. It's a way to connect to your authenticity, what makes you unique—**because no one else has lived your story.**

What most of us want is to feel more confident. We want to stand in our power and swagger in the room with such confidence and self-authority it oozes out of our pores like pheromonal musk. We want to know how to shake the feeling of being an impostor, a woman wearing a Chanel knockoff sitting at the Waldorf Astoria hotel bar, just waiting to get found out. That feeling sucks.

I've coached and creatively partnered with high-profile execs and successful creators who want to be able to rest confidently in themselves—past, present, and future. Like most things in life, no wonder drug will fill you with Logan Roy fuck-off confidence, but there is a beautiful practice that gives you a sense of deep confidence.

It's learning to trust yourself. You do that by not giving your power away.

You leak power when you:
- assume someone else knows what's right for you.
- allow other people to define you.
- follow someone else's idea of success.
- need to be validated by someone else to feel worthy.

I'm not saying don't learn from people, but trust you know what's right for you. There are tons of people to learn from; trust you know which ones to choose. Confidence comes from *knowing* and trusting yourself and shaking off ideas someone else—your mother, father, former boss, or ex—has about you, and writing your own stories about yourself. Maybe you messed up royally—welcome to the Human Club—but these mistakes show you that you *can* trust yourself because *you* got yourself out of that burning building. **Because if you got yourself here, you can take yourself there.**

You are already powerful. You have everything you need, right here, right now. If you don't believe your ideas are worthy of creating and sharing, you'll be stuck mirroring someone else. And that's the biggest source of impostor vibes. Because you are an impostor if you're wearing someone else's clothes hoping people recognize you. This might feel safe momentarily, but it's dangerous because you erode trust in yourself.

The remedy is to come home to yourself, to be so comfortable in your own clothes and quirky fashion sense that you wear your skin like it's Hermès. That's what attracts *your* people and differentiates you, because there is only *one* you in this world. So instead of spending your precious energy emulating someone else's way of living, get wildly curious about yourself. Find out what stories you're telling yourself about *you*.

Are they:
- outdated?
- inherited?
- helpful or harmful?
- *true*?

Look for proof and create evidence for the belief you're going to write about yourself:

• "I'm a badass creative."
• "My voice is unique."
• "I have magical shit to share."
• "I am in control of my own story."

Fill in the blanks.

It's not easy unraveling, revealing, disrobing, and expressing yourself, but it is immensely satisfying. It feels like your path, the one you were put here to walk, and that's meaningful. Trust is your compass. Without trust, there is no confidence, and without confidence, you won't walk *your* path. How much sweeter will success be—*or maybe that's success right there*—when you create and share from an authentic, raw *you* place and design your own way? That, my friends, is your ticket to freedom and fulfillment, and only you can give it to yourself.

If you can hand yourself a *Get Out of Jail Free* card, you were also the one who put yourself behind bars in the first place. In the next chapter, I'm going to get personal, sharing the story of my fractured marriage to show shape-shifting is more pain than pleasure, and the cracks that allowed me to see the wild beyond.

Fieldwork

Your lifeline: Your life story is a rich fabric stitched with meaning but it can be hard to see the patterns when you're on the ground. The lifeline exercise gives you a helicopter view of the unique series of significant moments that shaped your life.

Steps:
1. Get a blank sheet of paper. Draw a T on its side. Mark the horizontal line across the middle of the long part of a page. This axis is time—your life from birth to now. The vertical line is your experience—highs and lows.
2. Mark your age at different points on the line.
3. Plot key events: Put a dot for each event and label it. Place it high or low depending on your experience of it.
4. Draw a line connecting the dots.

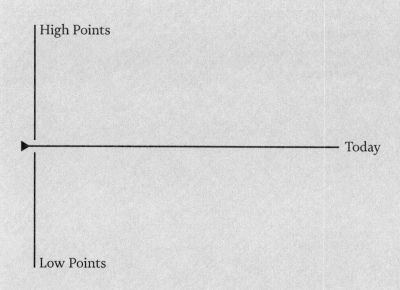

Reflect on your lifeline:

- What do you notice? Is there anything that surprises you?
- Are there any themes or patterns that emerged?
- What have been the key turning points?
- What experiences shaped you most? What have you learned about yourself?
- If someone looked at your lifeline, what would they say mattered to you?

Self-trust exercise: Reflect on every low point, how you overcame it, and where it led you. If you got yourself here, trust that you can get yourself there and handle whatever comes your way. That's your evidence.

A storytelling exercise

1. The past: What are the major milestones and struggles that led you to where you are now, in your business or creative venture?
2. The present: Write about your journey so far. What are you doing now?
3. The future: Write about the future that you envision as if it's already occurred.

silky snakeskins

He feels like Xanax and Valium combined. When I first meet Issam, I sink into his company like an old couch. His weight on the planet seems more solid than others. We're at a consultancy house in a small town in Belgium, where we wait to find out which country is ripe for an economic documentary to attract investment from all the venture capitalists watching CBS in the dead of night. As a recent *summa cum laude* grad from NYU's Center for Global Affairs, I'm filled with ideas about how to change the world.

When I have to choose between taking a contract role at the United Nations Development Programme's marketing and communication department in NYC or what I thought was scripting an economic documentary, code for selling ad space to produce a show in the Middle East, I picked the latter. Plus, the tenuous contract salary was a penance, considering the cost of living in New York and my hefty student loan.

Among the consultants passing time in the big house in Limburg, Issam and I gravitate toward each other, sun and earth style. He listens closely as I describe my thesis on the role of transitional justice in post-conflict peacebuilding and how *Battlestar Galactica* reveals our humanity as we bike under the light of antique street lamps through green fields, parking in grass that leaves zigzag tattoos on our elbow skin.

We watch *John Wick* together, Keanu Reeves bland as white bread, the sliver of space between our hands electric. I have no clue what that movie was about, but I remember how Issam's full lips turned into a wide, perfectly straight-tooth smile and his ambivalent relaxed presence. I wondered if this is a French attribute. When I asked him why he doesn't get excited about things, he responded, "I'm French. We don't get excited. We don't even have a proper word for *excited*." I learned that excitement is a very American trait.

One Friday night at the consultancy house where we all lived, a love child of a frat house and *The Real World*, bored media people bring out vodka as Gnarls Barkley sings "Crazy." I sit with John, ice cracking in my vodka Red Bull, his coy smile appearing through smoke, clinking his glass with mine. Issam's conspicuously absent, avoiding alcohol and the entire scene. Later, he tells me smoking is deadly and suggests I stop, which feels like kindness.

We spend our days together until they bleed into night and make out until our lips crack and mouths run dry. He carries me over the damp grass to my room, smiling as we cross a threshold together. Ten days later, I'm dispatched to Bahrain, and he's off to Dubai. We fall deeper in love over long emails and Skype, even as I spiral into the reality of selling ad space to CEOs and ministers, masking my last name and half Jewish background. If only masking gender was as easy.

After a long day of sales meetings with my Greek American partner, who's never without makeup, I meet the prince's cousin, Abbas, meaning "lion" in Arabic, at a party, and we laugh ferociously together, eyes twinkling under moonlight. While speeding down a sparsely lit road in his Ferrari, the police stop us, and he throws his royal identity card toward the officer to a stream of apologies in Arabic. We screech onward toward his house, where we'll smoke hash, drink scotch, and slow dance to the tracks he made, tongues rolling and roaring to the music.

I find myself in movie scenes and keep this cinematic world to myself: jumping off the yacht of the son of a Saudi financier, along with Emirates flight attendants, clinking glasses of Veuve while the sun bleeds into the sky. I meet Karim, the music director and resident DJ at Likqid Club, and we become fast friends, dancing to German techno and Arabic electronica until we're drenched from bubbly and sweat.

Issam makes it clear no partner of his would drink, yet I desperately want to be anchored to his steady calm. I become the version he needs me to be, a small price to pay for love, right? And who needs alcohol anyway? It just gets me into trouble. I need to get this out of my system and then we'll be together, and I'll become solid again.

During one of our late night calls, Issam says, "I need to talk to you about something that's been weighing on my mind." I suddenly get nervous and guilty, wondering if some juicy tidbit found its way to him. My body tenses, breath quickens. "I feel you'd have to give up too much to be with me. That wouldn't be fair to you."

The wind whips the sand against the window in the apartment we traded for air time on CBS. I quickly reply, "But we're in love. Isn't that what matters most?"

His version of love comes with terms and conditions. Mine means changing into a shape that makes me worthy of it, not realizing that loving myself in the original skin I'm in is the start of a *real* love affair.

He sighs. "I love you, and that's why I am telling you this. I'm afraid you'd come to resent having to change for me and my family."

Issam said the words, but I heard my mother's voice telling me we were moving, again, and me shouting that I wanted to stay. I couldn't let go of Issam, my anchor, or I'd be carted away again in the turbulent sea of all the years before him. I'd be swallowed by waves of chaos.

This was a chance to star in the after-school special. I needed a wardrobe change. This wild-black-rimmed-eyed, drunk yacht jumping, white tank top, and ripped jeans outfit wouldn't do. If I wanted to be accepted into his world, with its promise of a hand that doesn't let go, fingers that stay wrapped around mine, I needed to be another shape.

The old thought, *If I were different, maybe I could have kept my mother home*, appears. At this moment, I feel his fingers start to slip from mine, and I pull tighter.

"But I don't need it. I need you, and I love you. We'll figure the rest out together."

I was in a wild explosive state, and I had no idea how to contain myself. I never learned how to do that. I needed him to do it for me.

"If that's what you want, then of course we will."

And with that, his warnings went quiet. He offered me an out, and I signed the waiver that absolved him from being an accessory to my shape-shifting, trying to fit the mold he set on the table.

Six months later, we quit at the same time, flew to Strasbourg, and drove to the small town where his family lives. His father built the two-story house decades ago when they emigrated from Fes. The house faces a big, open field, surrounded by heavy figs and plums that fall to the ground and split open, releasing a honeyed, slightly nauseating scent that combines with soapy fresh lavender lining the stairs.

I moved into a room in the basement while we looked for jobs in London or Paris. I knit with his close Moroccan family. I slip in easily, snug in their daily rhythms. We laugh at French comedies, drive to Germany for ice cream sundaes, and haggle at the local farmer's market. We spent three months together, eating from the same Tagine plate on a U-shaped couch with a round table at its center every evening.

When Issam, his two sisters, and brother slowly come downstairs to the kitchen in the mornings, creased and wild-curled, everyone kisses each other on the right and then left cheek. I walk in the fields with his father, and he playfully chastises me for not greeting the farmer who passes us by. New York habits die hard. I make rosewater cookies with his mother and sisters, get the worst haircut in the only mall in the village and wail dramatically in the basement—to everyone's surprise—and clean out the debris of a past life.

At night, Issam sneaks into my room, and we make out like thieves. When he leaves, my stomach knots, memories of strobe lights flashing on the ceiling. The words of my friend Karim echoing in my head. "Are you really going to be able to live this kind of life?" softly adding, "Rules don't seem made for you. Or at least for you to break 'em." I toss and turn, putting the pillow over my head, trying to absorb the wild thoughts running free in the dark of the basement.

We finally both find jobs in London and move to Maida Vale, and life feels secure with the adventure of a new city and romance exciting and everything under control. Until tiny fissures start to appear. I find myself smoking cigs with colleagues at lunch when I was only an occasional social-drink-in-hand smoker, heading to the pub for a pint, and chewing a pack of extra strength peppermint gum before coming home. My stomach does cartwheels, chills running down my spine at the thought of a former shape slipping out and onto our bright kitchen floor.

One night, I come home from an agency pub crawl totally shitfaced—British women can drink me under the table, and I make the mistake of trying to keep up—and wake up to Issam, eyes rimmed with disappointment, showing photos of me hugging the toilet bowl, asking why I would want to do this to myself. I broke the contract, and he painfully reminded me of it. Instead of using his two hands to hold my hair, wipe my face with a warm washcloth, and carry me into bed, he held his iPhone, creating evidence of the breach, and left me in my underwear on the cold tiles.

When we're at home after work, cooking dinner together, binging Kiefer Sutherland in 24, and making love, we're steady, content. My old New York City clubbing partner in crime, Anna, calls to say she'll be visiting London. My chest clenches. "Please don't bring up any of our old partying stories when you meet Issam. Promise me, okay?" I put old snakeskins in a shoebox and slide it under the bed.

In the quiet of our fourth-floor walk-up and the warmth of our bed, Issam asks when we should get married, because it's a given between us, and the date is set for summer in Morocco. In London, we have an interview with a representative at the Moroccan consulate to register the marriage in Morocco. He asks me what religion I am—none, really—but I've been told I need to claim either Catholic like my mom or Jewish my dad in order to get the permission to marry since marriage to polytheists is not allowed. So I chose Jewish, which felt kind of poetic, a small way to heal the divide.

I imagine the wedding ceremony will be in the desert on carpets and in tents surrounded by camels, drum beats, candlelight, and mystery, and when I share this with my mother-in-law, she shakes her head. Issam explains I've described a Berber wedding, which is not part of their culture. I have no idea what a Moroccan marriage involves. I feel overwhelmed, out of my depth. His mother offers to plan the wedding— from the hammam day to the henna party, from catering to the seven gown rentals. I insist on wearing the wedding dress I bought in Arizona, but besides that, capitulate. I tell myself how much easier this will make it; that I get to focus on our wedding experience.

The dry wedding starts at 10:00 p.m.—it's too hot to begin earlier—and my wedding guests, my mom, dad, uncle, and closest friends, are holed up in their hotel rooms. They're suffering from a serious case of food poisoning from last night's chicken cooked in smen, a fermented and preserved butter that was rancid. Only me and my best friend Heather avoided that fate as a vegetarian and a vegan.

Despite my protests, I am layered thick in makeup, wearing the first of seven wedding kaftans, bright pink crusted with glittering gems, weighted by a fourteen-karat gold belt, reminiscent of boxing champions, and a golden crown. The bride is meant to outshine everyone in glimmering bright colors, a big departure from my New York City noir attire.

At the top of the stairs leading to the ballroom, I am announced by a high-pitched, joyful *zaghrouta*. With this Arabic *huzzah*, happiness courses through me as I walk down the stairs led by the wedding *negafa*, the woman who rented us the gowns and gold. She introduces me after each kaftan shift, keeping a close eye on my borrowed bling. I dance in the middle of the floor to the intoxicating beat of live Moroccan Chaabi folk music, hips swaying, arms in the air, henna hands moving softly and fluidly, the movement emanating from my wrists.

Issam dances next to me, his white jabador swaying, face damp and cheeks shining. The *negafa* glares at me, standing next to the white couch placed front and center in the room, which, I find out later, is where I am supposed to sit demurely. While dancing, his cousins asked us where I learned to dance Arabic style, or if I took lessons for the wedding. They don't know I'm a shapeshifter, able to easily slip into different skins and movements, but at this moment, on the dance floor, hips rolling to live drums, I'm in my original form—and free.

After living in London for two years in mostly steady bliss, the questions about baby making start coming in from different members of the family, especially my mother-in-law. I've never been pregnant, I fear I'll never be able to, and somewhere deep within, there's a part of me that wonders if I want to be. Even in my early thirties, I didn't have that maternal urge.

I feared with kids, my world with Issam would become even smaller, doors closing and locking. He made it clear that kids were a priority, a nonnegotiable. Family is what life is all about; adds an amendment to the contract. I thought his dreams could become mine.

I'm torn between thoughts—*I'm not sure I want kids or can even have them*—creating an internal churning and nausea. I mistake someone else's dog-eared script for safety, and it starts to feel dangerous, tight, and monotonous. This skin itches like a tight polyester suit, making me break out in hives. I pull on my collar, trying to breathe, but I can't seem to get enough air into my lungs.

When the opportunity for an agency interview in Copenhagen pops up, I fly to the city. Drawn to its tree-lined bike paths and dusty pink, blue, and orange buildings along a canal, and wowed by the creative director, we decide to relocate. It's a better place to raise a family than London. It would be another adventure, beyond the immediate pressure of further settling down.

I start going to after-agency parties, come home late at night, struggle with guilt and shame, afraid old wild parts will burst out *Mad Max*-style, and leave my life behind in smoke. The skin and script are too tight. I'm starting to claw at them. I don't know how to talk about it with Issam. I've never been one for binding contracts, yet I signed more than one. The only way out was to cut it into pieces like an expired credit card. Every night out with colleagues a snip of the script, a tear in my synthetic skin, a personal rebellion.

Something in me knew I had to break out. The more I go out, the more Issam retreats, closing like a Venus flytrap around himself. Our conversations strain like the yogurt his mom makes in the mesh hanging from the kitchen tap, stretched thin, words gone missing under laundry piles. Slowly, this intuitive wild starts ripping through the fabric, no longer willing to be contained.

On the night of a big *Mad Men*-themed agency party, I'm wearing a Betsey Johnson silk 1960s-inspired red and white polka-dot dress, leaving scarlet lip prints on martini glasses, and smoking cigarettes with a long black holder in the meeting room. Along with three colleagues, I performed a lip-synching number to "Zou Bisou Bisou," winning the *Mad Men* prize. Walking around the former 1952 factory building with its high ceilings and huge open space, looking at my colleagues dressed like late fifties ad execs, feels like we've jumped timelines into a new world. Laughter echoes, the bass thumps, lipstick bleeds, ties slacken, and brogues and heels stick to the cement floor covered in old fashioneds and crushed cherries.

Joachim, an art director, blond hair falling over his blue eyes, pulls me into the bathroom. We enter a stall and make out like hungry teenagers, our bodies against the steel wall. I get lost in the warmth of his mouth, our tongues snaking and undulating, celebrating their reunion, as if we had lost each other a long time ago, now finally found.

So begins the treacherous, grand, unconscious escape. I follow the only script I have to get out: creating chaos, imagining new worlds, moving fast, and moving on.

meat
a poem for escape artists

You stand behind the counter
white T-shirt rolled up
tight around sinewy biceps
cured meat swinging softly
over your just-rolled-out-of-bed head.

It's a family-run business,
but I see the way your hands
carefully wrap chicken
folding wax paper tenderly
over exposed breasts.

The gold cross around your neck
catches the sun streaming through windows
past cured olives and bathing mozzarella
revealing full lips, blue jean eyes
and dark runaway hair.

You flip the wooden counter open
wade through sawdust on the floor
that absorbs blood and your Drakkar Noir
to lift me up,
meaty hands find
where ass and thigh meet
(as if my body were bones
only you could read).

Your body slams into mine,
veins crawl over triceps
hands tear at my skirt
then release the clasp of my bra
in one stealth movement.

My nails scrape your shoulders,
our tongues collide, saliva flooding
the fleshy inside of cheeks,
your calloused fingers tightening around ribs
dipping into the membrane of desire
starving, we feed.

You delicately filet,
cut into the heart of me,
strip me down,
until I am tender enough
to really feel.

Your teeth bite into my neck
juices run down milky skin
that you mop up with your T-shirt,
a napkin that soaks, turns pink
a stain marking my spot.

For a moment, I forget the end of me
and the start of you.
The beat of our bodies brings me
to a place I haven't visited before
yet feels like home.

The door suddenly chimes opens,
rings louder than Taylor Swift
singing "You Belong with Me"

I am snapped back into place,
sweaty hand clutching the ticket,
still waiting for my number to be called.

hello there, good-looking
(meet your future self)

I threw an infidelity bomb at my marriage to escape in the smoke.
The distance growing between us, the feeling of being trapped, and
the fertility fear now covered in rubble. I blew it up instead of dealing
with it because I didn't know how, so I leaned on the old classic do-over
script. I quickly latched on to a toxic rebound who looked like an orange
lifebuoy in the middle of a dark sea. I was sputtering salt water, dog-
paddling five glasses of Sauvignon blanc deep to keep afloat and mask
the feeling of being in the wrong place, having no idea how to get out.
In therapy, I was learning how to stay, so I wondered, "How do you
know when to leave?"

Even though the rebound was painful, I didn't dare let go. I was scared
to be alone. It had been years since I'd been on my own. I lost touch with
that rebellious seventeen-year-old who left home with no idea what
the future would hold for her. I forgot how to swim after being caught
in the algae of others for so long. I forgot who the fuck I was. I had to
get lost to find myself again. It was time to let go of parts of me that
no longer served, leaving behind a long phosphorescent, delicate skin.
Because what got me here won't get me there. I had to imagine *there*, but I
was stuck trying to get out of *here*. I couldn't envision the future. I was
just trying *not* to drown, let alone get a view of the horizon.

When I got fired from a job I poured everything I had into, desperately
trying to make one part of my life work, it all started to fall apart. If my
life were a deck of cards, the universe had me play fifty-two pick-up.
Everything felt absolutely fucked. Sitting in the ruins of my job and
my shattered relationship, I had to look at the mess. Without a job,
my work visa would expire, and I'd have to leave Denmark within six
months. I had one lifeline—six months paid leave. Sitting among the
scattered deck, I played a different card. I decided to follow my gut and

bucket list desire to travel the Trans-Siberian Express and leave for a four-week trip across China, Mongolia, and Russia—alone.

When entering Mongolia from China, the trains switch, and I am transported back in time. I find myself in a cabin with plush burgundy and gold velvet seats. Instead of bright overhead lights, there's a soft lantern-style glow and a faint, earthy scent of wool and wood that mingles with freshly brewed tea. A print of wild horses running in the steppes hangs next to a taxidermized horned sheep. The gentle rhythm of the train, along with the chime of Mongolian music, makes me not want to get off until twenty-four hours pass and I'm so ready to disembark.

I decided to get off at Mongolia's capital, Ulaanbaatar, and make my way to the Gobi Desert. I quickly find out there's no way I can travel across a desert with no roads or signs without a guide. The host of the bed-and-breakfast, which is more like an extra room in their apartment, suggests finding someone to travel with, which would make the tour much cheaper. Luckily, there is another woman, Tomke, a German geology graduate student, looking for a travel buddy.

We pair up and head to the Singing Dunes, also known as Khongoryn Els, one of the largest sand dunes in Mongolia. If it's windy enough, when the sand shifts, it causes friction between the grains, which create vibrations that produce sound. Our guide speaks a bit of Russian and Mongolian, but no English. Body language goes a long way. When the towering dunes come into view, we're gobsmacked. They seem to stretch forever, or more accurately, for over sixty miles with heights of up to 984 feet. I want to climb to the top, watch the sun set, and hear those dunes sing. But that means climbing almost one thousand feet through the sand. How hard could it be? Only one way to find out. Tomke and I started the climb, despite the guide shaking his hands high in the air.

The sand, fine and uniform, undulates like waves under our sinking feet. The wind violently whips our windbreakers, hair flying out of ponytails and into our eyes, as grains find their way in between our teeth. All we can see for miles is rising golden dunes and an open expanse that's completely unpopulated. It's exhilarating. Until we reach halfway up the dune, and Tomke's legs are on fire.

"Pia, I don't think I can make it."

I stop, look back, and make my way to Tomke.

"You can. We can. I have a trick we can use that will keep us going."

Tomke looks at me wearily.

"We take ten big steps, then break. Ten big steps, then break. Together. Until we reach the top. Think of the bleeding sunset. Hearing the dunes sing. Just ten more steps. Okay?"

"Ja. Okay. Let's go. Together."

As we climb, the sand dunes start to release a deep hum and then a booming noise. We turn to look at each other with awe and grit in our eyes. We laugh on the breaks, sing along with the dunes, and keep climbing until finally we reach the top just as the sun is setting. The sun unfurls a blanket of gold, pink, and purple over the expanse of a desert so vast the horizon never ends, like an immense sea of sand. It's the most beautiful sunset I have ever witnessed. Tomke and I hug and smile until our cheeks ache, legs burning, lips chapped, sitting on top of an endless world.

I showed myself anything is possible, even in my early forties. Having nothing left to lose is the sweetest freedom.

The transformation from *here to there,* from feeling alone sitting on the couch with your partner to sitting on top of one of Mongolia's highest sand dunes, is mighty uncomfortable, sometimes downright painful, and difficult to be in. It feels like the teeth-crumbling dream is real, spitting enamel into the sweaty palm of your hand, a disintegration. Your death is also a rebirth, a reintegration, as you stretch from the past to your future like Bazooka over a pink tongue. Sometimes, you need to be who you are *not* to find out who you really are.

You might be wondering, *What does any of this have to do with meeting my future self?* Becoming and meeting your future self often requires an entry fee: letting go of old patterns and parts of you that keep you limited and in a loop; and becoming aware of fears keeping you in a chokehold. It requires leaving old parts of yourself behind, parts that outgrew their usefulness, in order to *embrace your becoming.*

Often, visualizing and embodying the future isn't linear or a breezy walk in the park, but it is an indispensable part of growth, change, and success (whatever that means to you). It can take you from feeling stuck and rudderless to free and connected to your inner compass. Imagining a bright future in a dark room might not feel easy, but it is in this fog that visualization has its most transformative potential. If you're in a velvety night, visualization makes way for constellations. And if the sun is warming your skin, visualization takes you to the next heart-throb island destination. Total win-win.

It doesn't have to be overly complicated. You don't have to go through years of therapy, experience heart-wrenching relationships, or rehash childhood trauma to shift into a new reality.

It starts with visualizing the future today.

According to the American Journal of Multidisciplinary Research and Innovation (AJMRI), visualization, also called visual imagery, is when we create a picture of what we want in our mind. Stated more formally for the doubters in the room, it is a specific process of applied neuroscience techniques to improve performance on any goal.[1]

Visualization is commonly used and widely accepted in the world of sports. Many athletes mentally rehearse the game in their head before they play, and it isn't just team sports that benefit from visualization. Michael Phelps, an Olympic gold medalist and swimmer, employs visualizations of his swimming events.

Research has shown that we stimulate the same brain regions when we *visualize* something and when we *actually* do it. A study found that "imagining moving certain parts of your body almost trains the muscles as much as the actual movement."[2] You still need to do the physical training along with the visualization exercise to make that happen, but when the two are combined, the result is amplified and magnified.

Studies show visualization increases the likelihood of success. Kobe Bryant was well-known for his work ethic, holding himself to shooting eight hundred shots before tipoff every night. What most people don't know is that some of Kobe's most important work was done alone in a quiet room with his eyes closed, picturing the game to be played, a practice shared by Michael Jordan. Even before he was given the honor, Jordan said he'd always imagined himself taking the game's final shot. "He saw himself in the biggest moments, making the biggest shots, and he was ready when the time came."[3]

> *"If my mind can imagine it and my heart can believe it, then I can achieve it."*[4]
>
> —Muhammad Ali

Athletes, entertainers, surgeons, doctors, police officers, and politicians all believe in the power of the mind. Affirmation and visualization are powerful tools used by celebrities—from Arnold Schwarzenegger to

Jim Carrey. When Jim Carrey was scraping to get by doing the comedy club circuit, he wrote himself a check to the tune of $10 million for acting services rendered. He dated it Thanksgiving 1995, and carried that crumpled, folded piece of paper in his wallet for years, sitting with his vision of the future every night. Three years later, just before Thanksgiving 1995, he found out he was going to make $10 million on *Dumb and Dumber.* **So, why not write your check?**

I wrote my first check on a somatic yoga retreat. In one of the exercises, we moved to music while the teacher invited us to imagine the future and feel it in the body. She asked sensory questions about this desired future as we grooved through a series of songs. "What does this feel like in the body?" "What do you see, touch, smell, hear, and feel?" "How can you fully embody that future now?"

Afterward, in the sunlight, grass between my toes, I journaled about the experience. I imagined having a creative studio, partnered with my person. I could hear his voice and feel the ache in my cheeks and the chill in my spine as we ate dinner in our summer house's garden. We're surrounded by friends, fairy lights twinkling, music and laughter drifting in the breeze. He touches the small of my back and asks me if I need anything from the kitchen while his kids hide and seek behind trees. Two years later, I met and then married my now husband, who has two kids, and eventually launched my creative studio.

After coaching certification, the check-writing visualization skill was supercharged, and I guide clients and myself to envision and embody the future. I don't only meet my future self; I merge with her. I visualize the contours, colors, and texture of my future, but most importantly, I connect to the *feeling* of it *now.* I see myself staring into the expanse of the desert from my front porch, hair sun-kissed, a pile of my freshly published books beside me, my husband bringing me a cup of coffee, feeling the warmth of him as he lays his hand on my shoulder. Stacked gold rings glimmer on my fingers, and a felt camel hat provides shade, my beige and black poncho flapping in the breeze along with the smell of creosote. I feel limitless, free, and deeply fulfilled.

The act of imagining and visualizing puts you in the creative director's chair. It makes clear what you *really* want and creates a sensory sketch and experience of that desired future in the present moment. It's easy to forget that you're the main player in this game of life. Sometimes, it can feel like life is happening to you and you're a victim of circumstance trying to catch curve balls randomly thrown at you, but you are also happening to life.

You're creating your reality in every moment. Or rather, reality responds to who you're being in every moment. If you are not consciously choosing which character you're playing, the default programming chooses for you. Are you the victim, the victor, the champion, the charmer, the rebel, the warrior, the poet, or the prince? Choosing who you are at any given moment is how you shape your reality.

When I was in a long-winded rebound relationship, my default childhood programming chose the shapeshifter, the one able to fit in any space and make the best of it, *forgetting* she gets to choose the space she wants to be in and the shape she wants to take. I had to become aware of the role I was playing to choose who I wanted to be.

Visualization is a felt sense of the future. You need to involve the five senses to feel the future in the body. It's both visual and sensory. As research demonstrates, "Visualization occurs when the mind imagines something, and the body responds." Emily Cook, a three-time Olympian, has said, "The word visualization, for me, does not take in all the senses. You must smell it. You must hear it. Everything has to be felt."[6]

Often, what we're after is not the goal itself but the *feeling* it will give us. When you want something *outside of* yourself, what you're really after is a feeling *within* yourself. We want to achieve or accomplish something to change the way we feel right now. The mainstream story goes: Do → Have → Be. But that will leave you peddling and sweating on the hamster wheel because that feeling, created by external shiny objects, doesn't last. This works well for capitalism but not for us because we're using the wrong operating system. Any real change requires you to be the person who feels free, confident, or satisfied *first*: Be → Do → Have.[7]

When you are being the future version of yourself who is free, who embodies the feeling of freedom, you do the work differently, with a different energy, which draws in what you want to *have*. You feel "it" in your body.

Often, I'm after the feeling of freedom. Freedom feels like being on a road trip, hair fluttering through the window, wind tickling fingers. Skinny-dipping in the sea, endless horizons and possibilities. Daytime matinees, laughter in the moonlight, coffee under the shadow of a palm tree, lost time, dream-filled Sunday naps. This is what I'm after— not just money or success loosely defined, but the feeling of freedom. Sometimes, it's simply reminding myself I can create that feeling of freedom *now*. I can sip a cup of coffee in the yard and watch the leaves dance with the wind. **It's not somewhere out there but in here.**

As you stretch, dream, and imagine the future, make it a practice to appreciate all you have and all you are right here, right now. If you visualize the future without appreciating the present, you will get stuck in the scarcity trap. The key is to bring together and hold both— the desired future and sweet present. The dumplings right in front of you and the General Tso dish on its way. When you appreciate the present and trust what you desire is coming, a deep, warm *thank-you* arises now.

But you need to set it all in motion. You need to sketch the outline, texture, colors, and contours of your future. Are we talking beige silk rippling in the Fiji breeze, cool coconut water in your hand, sunlight warming your legs, and an uninhibited view of frothy beer-crested waves? What does it feel like to put yourself there? What kind of person are you being while you are there? Are you inviting your highest self to radiate sunshine reggae vibes to those around you? Are you passing out love like Halloween candy? How generous are you in this future?

What if you could create that for yourself right now?

I've seen my clients experience this live—the desire for something, discovering that it is really a feeling, creating that feeling now, and then already having it. It's realizing you're an active architect in your life's design. You're always creating whether or not you want to, because that's the nature of this reality.

So, who are you choosing to be, and what future are you choosing to inhabit *today*?

Fieldwork

Visualize it
1. Capture the future you want in detail—engaging the five senses—in writing or imagery.
2. Imagine and *feel* the emotion of having that now.
3. Bring elements of that future into your present.
4. Take micro actions everyday toward that future.
5. Connect to the visualization daily.

This daily connection is key because when your future life and self have been felt enough times, your subconscious mind will start going to work for you.

Write your future bio
In a year from now, your favorite host is about to interview you for a famous podcast, and you need to send a short bio. Write one that captures who and where you want to be.

A conversation in the *future*
Ask a friend to play a time-traveling game where you imagine meeting each other on the street five years from now.

You've accomplished everything you once dreamed of in the past five years. You're living your best life. Take turns sharing the highlights in the past tense as if they've already happened. Speaking in the past tense shifts you into a state of knowing. Since it's already happened, it's easy for your subconscious mind to believe it's happened.

Have fun and play with it. Suspend judgment. Engage your curiosity and creativity. You can design this experience any way you want.

we run in creative packs

I'm wounded, bleeding on the page. My past stains the screen. I don't see red, just a blinking cursor and black pixels. Until my editor points it out on one of our weekly calls. Shanna's jet-black hair and blue eyes pop on the screen, as pronounced as the pride flag on her bookshelf and printed skull on the tote bag hanging from her door. She enunciates words clearly, elocution on point, a remnant of her old theater days.

Directing her intense focus my way, she says, "You repeat yourself in your writing, finding different ways of saying the same thing. Even though the prose is beautiful, it's redundant. Pick the most powerful one and cut the rest."

I lean back in my knockoff Danish design white pleather office chair, my bookshelf mirroring hers. "Funny, I remember one of my professors at Hunter College giving me the same feedback. I wonder where it comes from?"

As a talented horror writer, maybe Shanna's gifted with the power to see how pain transmutes and speaks in different tongues, because what she says next floors me.

"Well, for one, your copywriting background factors in, driving a message home through repetition, but, from reading your book, I think it comes from not being seen as a child."

A punch in the solar plexus. A shot of deftly administered truth serum wakes me up to the repetitious pattern. She sees me and helps me see myself so I don't impose my duplications on you, dear reader.

Writing this book reinforces what I discovered after more than a decade of working in the creative industry: Creativity *is* collaboration.

It further smashes the lone creative genius myth that sticks to culture like a sheet of fabric softener on a freshly dried tracksuit. The old script of the lone author in a cabin in the woods, working on his craft through his solitary genius, stopped me from even attempting to write a book. Where would I start? How would I manage this massive undertaking by myself? Turns out, like every other creative venture, I didn't have to. Because, like vampires and unicorns, there is no such thing as a lone creative genius. So why is it so pervasive?

Historically, the lone creative genius is a recent idea. "Prior to the Enlightenment, individuals were rarely referred to as 'geniuses.' Rather, they *had* geniuses—as in, supernatural or divine forces that gave them their ideas and creativity."[1] Harvard scholar Marjorie Garber explains that "genius" meant "a tutelary god or spirit given to every person at birth."[2]

The Greeks famously called these divine creative spirits "daemons." Socrates believed he had a daemon who spoke wisdom to him from afar. The Romans had the same idea, but they called this disembodied creative spirit a "genius." They believed a genius was a magical divine entity who would invisibly assist the artist and shape the outcome of her work. This view changed with the Renaissance, when the individual human being was placed at the center of the universe above gods and mysteries. People started to believe creativity came from the individual. For the first time in history, you started to hear people referring to the artist as being a genius, rather than having a genius.[3]

Whether it's Jobs, Picasso, or even Queen Bey, the belief that brilliant individuals—rather than teams of hardworking, talented people—are behind the world's most significant creative breakthroughs is seductive. "The idea that there are near-Gods of creativity among us is a potent one, particularly in a world that feels increasingly unpredictable; if we can't have the stability of God, at least we might have people who appear to approach something close to it."[4]

The lone genius myth is not only outdated but harmful. It caused 2008 Nobel Prize winner Martin Chalfie to abandon his early scientific career. According to Chalfie, his first experience with science ended badly because he was too afraid to ask for help. The stories he'd heard about great scientists were of lone geniuses who made their breakthroughs without the help of others. He thought that if he was cut out to be a scientist, he should be able to do his experiments entirely by himself.

Chalfie said, "I felt that I had to do everything on my own, because asking for help was a sign that I was not intelligent enough. I now see how destructive this attitude was, but then I assumed that this was what I had to do."[5]

Creative genius is also inextricably wrapped up in societal biases.

A study debunked the myth of the lone genius by exploring "the problematic nature of a hyper-individualistic understanding of creativity." The research highlighted how creativity has historically been viewed as a rare, natural talent only possessed by a gifted few—especially white, Anglo-Saxon men. This white ethnocentric and male-dominated way of seeing the world resulted in prioritizing stories that reinforced this narrative while ignoring those that didn't.[6]

Steve Jobs, who many refer to a modern day creative genius, provides us with more recent evidence of this persistent myth. Sure, he was indispensable to Apple's success, but too often the work of cofounders Steve Wozniak and Ronald Wayne got sliced from the narrative. This myth also plays out in the case of Jeff Bezos. The media omits the role MacKenzie Scott played when she joined the risky start-up and did the accounting and negotiated numerous contracts, making it seem as though Bezos had operated alone.[7] **The stories we're told perpetuate the myth that success is a solo affair.** Enough already.

Creativity is not a solitary act

The best work, the most beautiful creations or scientific breakthroughs—from NASA voyages to the Sistine Chapel—is the product of working together. Michelangelo painted the Sistine Chapel with the help of a team of assistants. "Even Einstein, perhaps the most iconic genius in history, didn't come up with his ideas in a vacuum." It was only after he spent years working in a Swiss patent office poring over other people's inventions that he made his mathematical breakthroughs.[8] Just watch the credits roll after any movie.

We stand on the shoulders of giants right out the gate. Everything we have, stories and inventions, we've inherited. We are constantly regurgitating, remixing, consuming, and building on the ideas and inventions of others. In her book *The Architecture of Influence: The Myth of Originality in the Twentieth Century,* Amanda Reeser Lawrence argues the ability to copy something, like a musical sequence or a brand logo, and add your own twist is an art form unto itself. She writes that Michelangelo, who many would consider a creative genius, learned by copying.[9] With advances in technology, from social media to AI, we can collaborate in real-time in ways we never could have imagined.

The real secret to creative success is believing, seeing, and experiencing how we're better together, and then rewriting that old and tired lone creative genius myth together (here's a pen). We build better businesses, dream bigger, grow taller, and solve complex problems *together.* I've experienced the magic of working collaboratively. I've witnessed ideas bubble and take flight in teams. Throughout my creative career, the best work has come from teams of art directors, designers, developers, and copywriters partnering with passionate clients to creatively solve commercial problems, not from lone creative geniuses. Often, those egos sink the ship and sour the work.

Creativity is a team sport

It's early November 2023. The bushes in my backyard got the pumpkin spice memo from Starbucks, their leaves deep orange, brown, and cream. I'm at the start of the book creation process, having just finished its outline. I lay on the cold floor in the kitchen, which, for some reason, calms my nervous system, and stare at the ceiling, listening to synths combine with the swooshing of the dishwasher.

This next phase of writing is fundamental, the genesis; it's where, working with a developmental editor, I will carve and craft the bones of the book. The spirit of my book whispers, "We need the right partner." I sit up, take a swig of kombucha, grab my laptop, and look at editors in the program. I see Shanna's photo and immediately feel called in, like those 1950s sitcoms where the mom opens the backdoor and yells, "Alice, it's time for dinner!"

I'm drawn to her bio, and after reading that she's worked with so many authors she's lost count, wrote *Miss Infection USA*, and sits on the diversity, equity, and inclusion committee, I'm hooked. I write the head of editing, Michael, and request to work with her. He replies in a text message, "We endeavor to pair people with the best editors, but we don't allow authors to choose." The gut feeling gnaws at me. I keep checking my messages to see if editors have been assigned yet and can't help but worry. I attend one of Shanna's classes to see if I'm fabricating the feeling, and our live exchange is the final pull that wins the tug o' war game.

When I finally receive the news that I've been paired with someone else, I deflate like a clown's failed animal balloon attempt. Following Michael's suggestion, I give the editor a chance, but every sign points to Shanna. I hound Michael until he caves.

After profusely thanking my intuition for leading me to my creative partner, our work together begins, and what I once thought would be a grueling solitary process transforms into an electric cocreation.

"There are three signals that someone is ready for a creative partnership," Shanna says. "First is curiosity. Do they believe they know how the project will turn out, or are they open to the process? Openness is essential. Then, vulnerability. Can we lock hands, trust one another, and skip toward the dark forest (where all the stories that matter live)? Willingness to create from that deep place is crucial. The third is something outside of our control but will come when the work is right: goosebumps. There's no explanation. The goosebumps always come on cue when a breakthrough is happening."

I have no idea our partnership will call forth past experiences that show how I moved from living life on autopilot to creatively directing it. Turns out, those are often raw, tender, and vulnerable stories. Shanna admits she put me through the wringer. "I asked Pia hard questions in the creation of this book. Trauma, death, and divorce were on the table. I'm not a therapist, although I do moonlight as a cheerleader when my authors are in a slump. My questions were in service of the story."

There is power in being witnessed. Shanna tucks a pencil behind her ear, gazes at me through her black-rimmed glasses and the screen, and says, "Anyone writing about something hard is going to dance around it."

"What's important about writing something hard?"

"Vulnerability creates a real connection between the author and the reader. These hard things often reveal universal truths we can all relate to."

"Like divorce?" I wink at her, knowing full well she pulled out deeper stories from me when I wanted nothing more than to skirt the surface.

"It's also what makes the book stand out. We all have a 7-Eleven within, so what makes the stock different is your unique wrapping and life experience. Everything's been written, but no one has experienced life the way you have."

Something magical happens when we create in pairs. "There is this potent creative force when two people get together and make something," Shanna says. "It's a force that, sometimes, shoves the author out of their own way."

While writing this book, I hear Shanna's voice, *Create the scene, draw people in. We, the readers, don't care about what Present Pia thinks about Past Pia's experience. We want to feel what she felt then.* We collaborate beyond video calls, her husky, cackling laughter entering the scene when I hesitate to murder darling prose.

"At its heart, the creative process is a push and pull between two people, two entities, two cultures, or even a single person and the voice inside her head," says Joshua Wolf Shenk, author of *Powers of Two: Finding the Essence of Innovation in Creative Pairs*. "The core experience described by the muse-creator interaction—that of one entity helping to inspire another—is almost always true."[10]

I get curious about the origin of "muse" and stumble upon this definition from Encyclopaedia Britannica, "Muse, in Greco-Roman religion and mythology, any of a group of sister goddesses... They probably began as the patron goddesses of poets."[11]

When our developmental editing process ends, and a new creative collaboration chapter opens, it hits me: We are each other's sister-goddess-muse. Or, as we'll hear Shanna put it: We take turns being the artist and the muse, the muse and the artist. In honor of the theme of this chapter, Shanna's experience deserves its own section.

Two humans floating on a space rock: Shanna's take on cocreation

Up late with my laptop running hot on my thighs, I work through Pia's early drafts. Keys click fast. I've edited for years. It comes easy, and I love the work, but it's getting too late and my eyes burn. Yet I slow, reading line-by-line, and stop typing. Goosebumps crawl up my arms. Pia wrote: "Creativity is not just something we do; it is how we respond to the challenges in life." My stomach growled. I didn't know I was starving for these words until she served them to me.

Unbeknownst to Pia, I'd frozen myself out of my own creativity for over two years. My fingers ached to write, but when poised above keys, nothing happened. Not through lack of trying! Endless hours were spent typing, deleting, writing, erasing, repeat, repeat, repeat. Yet, in the blueish laptop light, staring at Pia's words, a new thought was born: What if I'm always creative? What if I'm still a writer, an artist, even if I'm not producing work for my agent to sell? My mind knotted and unknotted itself (and a star Big Banged itself into existence).

Then, a few lines down: "You are in constant creative response with your experience." I nodded. Yes. Yes! I was in constant creative response with my experience. I was an artist, always and forever. It couldn't be taken from me. Words scribbled or blank page; it didn't matter! And if I wanted, I could change the course of my creative expression. I could write again or not. It was my life that was the art (and the star expanded into a stormy planet).

I typed up my editorial comments but didn't share that I'd had my own breakthrough. The energy between us flowed in one direction: downstream from editor to writer. No salmon swimming upstream on this planet—yet. But I furiously edited, devouring each chapter for the sake of her art and my own.

And I did write again, soon after. What flowed through the ink of my new pen was as alien as the surface of this new planet. I opened the spigot, and poetry poured out. Not the fiction my literary agent wanted to see, but that didn't matter. I put on a spacesuit and left my boot prints all over that gorgeous, terrifying landscape. My creativity flourished in my life as well, as I began to practice being an artist all the time, not just when writing. I got new tattoos for the first time in thirty years.

After sixteen weeks and a completed first draft, it's "break-up day," the final meeting between author and editor. I finish my intended to-do list for the meeting and pause. I don't want to "break up." I can't describe why our creative partnership is so exceptional. I can only feel it and see, through Pia's manuscript, what we could accomplish together. What could *I* create with the powers of her and me? What could *we* create through collaboration? There is no "Off" button on a volcano. You must let it run its eruptive, planet-forming course. After all previous formalities ended, I told her how her book and our partnership had shifted tectonic plates in my life.

She didn't want to let go either. So, we removed money from the equation, and I proposed a barter: continued editing through the final draft of the manuscript in exchange for coaching. I wanted everything I'd read in the book—all the fieldwork and bolded statements and poems—to enter a space that was sacred for me and my own work. Masks off. Money and contracts gone. Two humans floating on a space rock, taking turns being the artist and the muse, the muse and the artist.

Months into this terraforming venture, and I've fundamentally changed. Pia awakens a cast of characters inside of me that I call upon whenever I need. Their voices guide me to my gut, my purpose, and my creative future—just as she envisions in the pages of this book. I've already lived it before it's even been published.

The spirit of creativity

Shanna and I cocreate gravity that holds our planets, stars, poems, prose, texts, and tears together. Our shared vulnerability, curiosity, and connection breaks down the barriers of space and time, and we create wildly in our void.

Shanna brings out my bruises, a raw tenderness, and teenage bravery to show the story of a life lived creatively. She coaxes stories of how I lost and found my creative power onto the page. Like a daemon, she assists my inner artist and helps shape my work. But she's not the only one.

The spirit of my book visits me at night. It drops ideas in my dreams and rustles my hair playfully when I am writing. In the beginning, I tried to tightly define the book theme, and it rebelled, only allowing the answers to reveal themselves as I write, not before. As I move from chapter to chapter, it invites me to chisel the marble until the figure emerges and I let go of the image of David. As Michelangelo said, "Every block of stone has a statue inside it, and it is the task of the sculptor to discover it."[12]

I don't know where this creative force comes from, and frankly, I don't care. Being part of this kind of entangled creative collaboration is profoundly satisfying, like opening a can of Coke on a sweltering summer's day. It's beyond me, not from me. It's part of the collective energy that happened to choose me to write this book. "Vincent van Gogh famously told his brother Theo that his paintings weren't something he owned and that the creative process was part of the human experience and creation as a whole, not just one man."[13] Vinnie knew what was up.

Fieldwork

Look at different areas of your life: Where are you going at it alone, when you could be partnering up?

Struggling with an idea or problem?
Grab a partner and cocreate.

velour revolutions

I'm going to break my own rule in the spirit of this chapter. We're going to look at capital C creatives, a.k.a. artists. Breaking convention, taking risks, and following the syncopated beat of your heart and gut are essential to living a creative life. No one shows this more than creative giants.

There is a path carved by those who came before us, but it's just made up by someone, not handed down from the gods. The usual drill is marching from university to career, from family to retirement. But what if there's another way? What if you could reconnect to what really moves you and design a life experience that has you firing on all cylinders? If you're reading this book, I'd wager your (creative) rebel inside is shaking and rattling your rib cage.

Betsey Johnson, the iconic eighty-two-year-old fashion designer, known for what she calls "pretty and punk," sits on the patio of my Airbnb. We're in Tucson, where I'm visiting my father, who she dated before I was born. They were a creative powerhouse couple, sharing ideas about each other's art, both riding an artistic high. In 1971, Betsey became the youngest designer to receive the prestigious Coty Award,[1] and that same year, my dad exhibited his work at the MoMA.[2] They've been close—for more than fifty years—ever since.

As she sips coffee with sweetener, marking her mug with fire engine red lipstick, bright yellow and white blonde hair extensions framing her face, I find myself wishing for the same energy, life force, and beauty when I am in my early eighties.

I pull my chair a little closer, turn the volume of my phone up so we drown the chirping Cactus Wren, and ask, "What does creativity mean to you?"

Her long red nails click the mug. "Being alive is a creative existence. Whether you bake a pie or shovel your driveway pretty; it's all creative. It's your expression, and nobody else can do it like you. Your life is a creative force. Then it's what you do with it."

Immediately curious, I follow up with, "How did you know what you wanted to do with it?"

"I knew I didn't want to be like anybody else. I had to create my own expression—having no idea what category that expression was going to be in. Then I found my category: doing what I want. It amazes me how far out some of my stuff was, and I got away with it. Because somehow there was a far-out-enough girl who got it. But I didn't know that there was that girl. I wanted to experiment. I didn't want to copy anyone."

Betsey definitely found and established the heck out of her category. Working as the in-house designer for the youth culture punk boutique Paraphernalia in New York City in the mid-1960s, she flirted with and romanced rebellion in her life and designs. Through her work at Paraphernalia, she made costumes for the Velvet Underground.[3] In 1968, she married the band's founding member, John Cale, in her underwear after a city hall judge told her "women weren't allowed to marry" with pants on.[4]

Even though Betsey is all her own, her designs speak to many. Perhaps because she creates from a deeply sincere and intentional place, her creations have universal appeal; I imagine Martians donning frills and leopard prints. Instead of focusing on what the industry wanted, she had her eyes set on what women—her Betsey girls—wanted. Her designs were affordable, and Betsey was happy, fun, accessible, and unpretentious, which ran counter to fashion culture. According to *Paper Magazine*, "Perhaps being an outsider is what makes Johnson so fabulous."[5]

I ask her what's important when you're starting out. "It was realizing and knowing I'm from middle-class, local, normal, real people. A real dad with a foundry job, real mom working as a high school guidance teacher. I basically make clothes for myself. I realized that unless I can see somebody walking down the street and it's my dress they have on, what good is it? That was the thrill."

"I never wanted my designs to cost more than a round trip to Puerto Rico. That's what I based my price range on. I always had a job where I had $99, and I loved going to Puerto Rico for two nights." Betsey bounces her black, fuzzy, teddy-look Birkenstock sandal on her leg. "I realized I didn't have to stick to rules one through nine. I had rules nine through twelve that I could create."

"For the nineties, my fashion show days were just about not going by any of the rules, showing the clothes the way I wanted to."[6]

—Betsey Johnson

The Sonoran sun rises higher, and we break for water. We both prefer feeling the heat to being inside in a dark air-conditioned room, so we stay under the shade of the awning. Hearing Betsey's story is inspiring, but getting a chance to experience her energy as she tells her story, stands up and does a dance move, and says "Ta-da," speaking with her hands and with passion, pizzazz, humility, and humor, is what's really moving.

As we sit back down surrounded by cacti and a statue of the Buddha, I ask Betsey, "Did creativity help you overcome personal challenges in life?"

She bats caterpillar eyelashes, her dusty blue eyes fixed on me. "I still don't accept that I'm special and unique. I'm very insecure and worried, total Connecticut. I drummed up my confidence through experimentation. In the sixties, I lived in the Chelsea Hotel in New

York City for years. I'd put on my thing, whether it be a far out LSD scene outfit or little Paraphernalia dress I had to sell, and would use myself as the experiment, the guinea pig. I'd go to the Chelsea lobby and sit. I learned everything from just sitting and watching the response to me. And then you get it."

As an award-winning fashion icon, recently presented with the Geoffrey Beene Lifetime Achievement Award from the Council of Fashion Designers of America, hearing Betsey's self-doubt is unexpected and refreshing.[7] It underlines a vulnerability that connects us all and speaks to why she permeated culture and the lives of women around the world for over fifty years.

"Some people think when you're a creative person like me that creativity never ends; it always goes on. They gotta know everyone gets writer's block. That's part of it all. Creativity can be scary, especially when you don't have a clue. And I'm too used to success, financially and personally, and I don't want to do something that isn't great."

But you know she will do something great, especially when you hear her response when I asked what advice she'd give someone who yearns to live a more creative life.

"Understand that you don't know, but at least you're going to start. That's what I'm going through right now. I don't know where to put my creativity. I'm creative all the time, the way I tie my skirts, the way I get myself together, but I need to make something. And I have a feeling I'd go back to being five years old. I remember doing a *Sesame Street* show. Whatever you loved doing when you were little is hopefully what you end up doing when you're big."

What we are naturally drawn to, what we love, holds the key to our fulfillment and fun. It's what we've been coded to create. Some might call it destiny; others purpose. Whatever name you give it, that desire is uniquely yours and will, by definition, look different from what's out there. It will take courage and a splash or bucket full of rebellion to live that purpose and natural instinct and follow it through as its expression develops and shifts over the years.

> *"The most radical act of rebellion today is to relearn how to dream and to fight for that dream."*[8]
>
> —Nadezhda Tolokonnikova

Betsey's inner rebel spoke loud and clear. "I wanted my own independence. I did not want to be dependent on a job I didn't like. I never wanted a boss. I had to have my own way with everything. Paraphernalia had no rules. Designers just did their own thing, never told what to do or how to do it, only when to do it."

Creativity requires agency and bravery. A study conducted by leading creativity researcher and neuroscientist Nancy C. Andreasen found that creative people are adventuresome and exploratory, and their best work tends to occur in new frontiers. They take risks, face doubt, and deal with rejection. Yet, they keep going because they believe in what they do. Her study also revealed that "creative people work much harder than the average person," usually because they love their work.[9] When you are doing something you love, you lose time and enter a flow state. It doesn't feel like work.

As Nadezhda Tolokonnikova, founding member of Pussy Riot, writes, "Art requires hellish amounts of concentration and self-discipline, and you're totally in charge—there's nobody around to tell you what to do. There are no safety belts. No insurance or guarantee. But that's where the edge is."[10]

What do creative rebellions look like? Questioning and reexamining conventions and circumstances. Usually, we don't have time to challenge or contemplate because our minds are distracted by notifications, responsibilities, dinner plans, and grocery lists. It took a global pandemic to make us pause and get off the treadmill. This shifted something within many of us. It was a collective WTF moment that led to a reevaluation of our partnerships, jobs, and lives. We're still searching. The search itself is an act of creative rebellion, a defiant "I'm not going back to business as usual."

Capital C creatives are far from the only rebellious ones, because art doesn't sit outside your life. Your art is your life. The operative word is "your." It takes courage to make life your own, to not follow the prescriptive path carved by family or society. According to Alfred Balkin, educator and composer, "Creative risk-taking is not about dangerous or risky behavior, but an orientation to the new and to learning through mistakes or challenges."[11]

This requires loosening the grip on certainty, not waiting for the right, "safe" moment to do the thing. When I retire, when I have saved X amount, when I have another job lined up, then I'll take that trip, quit my job, write that book, and allow myself to enjoy life unguardedly. The right time is always now (to eat the avocado). The fear of survival, whether real or imagined, keeps us small and creatively risk-averse.

Yet risk helps us think more creatively. When we're in high-stakes, uncertain conditions, "the brain's pattern recognition system starts hunting through every possible database to find a solution."[12] The brain's intuitive creative system takes center stage, putting aside its rational extrinsic system. Risk trains the brain to think in unusual ways and be more creative. This doesn't mean throwing common sense out the window and jumping without a parachute, but it does mean getting uncomfortable as you move in the direction of what matters to you.

"When you make music or write or create, it's really your job to have mind-blowing, irresponsible, condomless sex with whatever idea it is you're writing about at the time."[13]

—Lady Gaga

Creative rebellion is refusing to take life as it has been handed to you. It's not following defined pathways because it's what everyone else is doing or says you *should* do. It's not believing the hype that to succeed, you must conform to norms or follow someone else's sage and sound advice. It's not accepting the stories you're told about how life needs to be lived. Creative rebellion is writing and living your own story, one that makes every cell in your body come online.

I am not what happened to me. I am not the stories I tell myself. I am not my thoughts. I am not a passive bystander. I will not eat everything I'm served, nor finish my plate. I refuse to sit in a box with a label on it. I will not toe the line, be nice, or be quiet. I am unquantifiable, untamable, limitless, formidable, in the world but not of it. I am a never-ending story. I am directing this goddamn show and eating only blue M&M's. I'll fuck and say "fuck" when I want to.

I will rock the cruise ship until champagne crashes on the deck, glasses shattering in tiny shards, hair loose and wild, freed from Aqua Net. I will not place my value on anything other than my spirit and humanity. I will build my pirate ship and choose my own adventure while wearing a rose-embroidered corset, black tutu, and an eye patch. This is a velour revolution.

"I think we're all creative," Betsey says, "but there's something scary about going to the creative world, financially and personally scary, so creativity can just be too scary to give it a shot. Especially when you don't have a clue. The way through it? Don't think about it, don't worry about it, just do it."

That's how you take risks for what you're called to create in the world. "There is a deep and meaningful connection between risk-taking and creativity, and it's one that's often overlooked," contributor Steven Kotler wrote in *Forbes*. "Creativity requires making public those bets first placed by imagination. This is not a job for the timid."[14] It is a job for the brave. It takes a velour revolution to find your own way and design your own experience.

Making life your art is the rebellious work of a lifetime.

the morning after

a poem for protagonists

The day-after-sweat soaks my bralette as I tap laptop keys, writing a new story, words easing from me like hot whispers in the dark. I flip my hair, releasing the scent of stale cigs, bringing last night into the morning light. A flash of us raising chipped mugs, "special" coffee spiked with bottom shelf vodka, grinning madly under the neon OPEN 24-HOURS sign in the diner window. Wet feral eyes, malnourished hearts, and fermented dreams in a red booth. The way the cross on your chain drags along your tongue. We share secrets and french fries, give each other static shocks, vinyl squeaking. Bite ketchup-stained bottom lips. My bubblegum pink toenails pressed between your blue jeans. Chiseled jawlines, exposed collarbones, sticky french toast tongues, and inky numbers on a diner napkin trick me into believing this night will never end.

But it does.

I throw the crumpled paper into the bin and miss. Perspiration remains my only link to you.

your life manual

I've taken the *Mad Men* theme too far. Leaning against the wall at the agency, I crush the Marlboro Light in the gold ashtray. I pluck the olive from my martini glass and chuck it directly into my mouth to avoid smudging cherry-red lipstick. When the tall blond art director I danced with grabs my hand and leads me to the bathroom, I don't object. The white-tiled walls muffle the music and chatter and chill the air.

Goosebumps erupt on my skin. Only porcelain sinks, steel doors, and open factory windows surround us. In my 1960s-inspired polka-dot dress and his black suit, we're different people in a different place, so the kiss that follows slips between the time and space crack. When I wake up the next morning, the diamond ring tight around my finger, I'm nauseous and clammy, soaked in shame and vodka. Being out of alignment with my values makes me dry heave, giving me the shakes and sweats.

I was in my late thirties, confronted by my infertility. Issam wanted nothing more than a family. A quiver in my bones told me I couldn't give him one. My stomach was often in knots. I started socially smoking again, numbing anxiety as I reached the bottom of wine glasses. I had no idea how to talk about this with him or to even meet it within myself. Did I even want children? Everyone seemed to agree babies were a good idea, but I was not convinced. I felt inadequate, defected, broken, and lost. The threat of multiple losses gave me heartburn.

I fell into an old pattern. In that bathroom stall, I tumbled down a rabbit hole that took me far away from my marriage. After my divorce, I almost moved to Paris, landing a role at another agency, but the visa process took forever. The communication from the agency was terrible, which put me off, so I decided to go to therapy instead.

In session, my therapist asks, "You've learned how to leave, but have you ever learned how to stay? To experience what it is like to get to know yourself, other people, and a place differently, deeply?"

The penny drops and reverberates within. It's the first time I even considered I had a choice. Moving, drama, and chaos kept me so busy, entertained even, I didn't have space or time to consider my choices, let alone my purpose. I confused purpose with pattern. I woke up when I became aware of the choice. I rewrote the script from "life is happening to me" to "life is happening through me."

I am a powerful creative designing my experience. And so are you. We don't get a manual for this thing called life, but we get to write our own. Its narrative is driven by two things: our purpose and our values.

Most of us don't realize stopping, stepping back, and creating our own guidebook is even a possibility. We're just following the script passed down to us, playing the role to the best of our ability. But we *can* make it our own. You can order that black fabric director's chair with your name on it (or is it just me who always wanted one of those?) and start directing, producing, and starring in the film that is your life. You get to choose the soundtrack, the cast of supporting characters, the set, the dialogue, the story, the plot. But first, you need to become aware of the script you're reading from.

I was reading that "creative freedom comes with a hefty price tag" script. When I was eight years old, I saw that drama play out.

My dad curls his bills into a tube, securing them tightly with a rubber band. He paints during the day and deals cards at night, watching men sweat and lose the deeds to their houses. He tells me stories of smoke-filled rooms ripe with desperation and riddled with hope. My mother works as a chef, and along with another partner born in March, creates Les Poissons, a catering company. She caters Rupert Holmes's release party for the "Escape (The Piña Colada Song)," and she never makes a single piña colada ever again.

I wear a key around my neck and walk home from P.S. 321 in Brooklyn. I come home to my mom wearing a stained apron, smelling like pâté, onions, and Chanel N°5, "The Girl from Ipanema" playing in the background, a glass of red wine in hand, head lost in the cloud of a joint, rubbing off the day like the chicken she massaged earlier.

I carried the hidden belief that "making money is hard" and "creativity doesn't pay the bills" for years. Luckily, my purpose was more ingrained than that tired old story and kept me on the creative track, even if in the commercial realm of advertising and marketing.

We're all driven by purpose. Reconnecting to what really moves you is deeply satisfying rocket fuel. Whether you identify your purpose or not, you will be living it, just not consciously. *So why bother?* Purpose is your North Star. It lights the way. Even when you're not sure where you're going, you know you're moving in the right direction, guided by what you feel uniquely driven to do in this world.

Purpose is not a vision, mission, or tightly defined objective. It's broad, inspirational, grandiose, flowery even, and somewhat abstract. Actually, whatever it sounds like to anyone else doesn't matter, because it is uniquely *yours*. What matters is that it resonates deeply with you. No one else needs to "get" it. Purpose motivates, guides, steers, and unsticks you. It's a big neon sign that helps you find your way out of a dark night of the soul. It helps you make decisions and ensures your ladder is against the right wall. Purpose is fueled by the desire to create an impact in the lives of others.

> *"The two most important days in your life are the day you are born and the day you find out why."*[1]
>
> —Mark Twain

You sense when you are "on" or "off" purpose. When you are on purpose, it feels deeply satisfying. When you are not on purpose, it feels off, like pushing against instead of leaning into. It's hard to shake the tightness in the pit of the stomach and shoulders and that suspicion you're off track. I felt that contraction for years in my post-divorce rebound relationship, but I wasn't ready nor brave enough to follow it, so the nagging and poking followed me.

When you're on purpose, the body feels expansive, like a deep exhalation. It's an inner knowing, the goosebumps or chills that come from being in the right place, even when the external might not yet reflect your purpose. Despite circumstance, a calm washes over you.

Purpose is life-affirming and extending. Research shows that finding your purpose is linked to living longer. A strong life purpose is defined as "a self-organizing life aim that stimulates goals." Researchers found that older adults who did not have a strong sense of meaning in their lives "were more than twice as likely to die… compared with those who had one." Specifically, they were more likely to die of cardiovascular diseases. These results were not limited to a specific group but universal, even when controlled for income, race, gender, and education level. They concluded that finding purpose not only helps people live longer but is essential for happiness and fulfillment.[2]

Modern scientific research on human purpose can be traced back to the harrowing experiences of a Holocaust survivor. Viennese psychologist Viktor Frankl observed that prisoners with a sense of purpose exhibited greater resilience to the horrific conditions. "Writing of his experience later, he found a partial explanation in a quote from Friedrich Nietzsche, 'Those who have a *why* to live, can bear almost any *how*.'"[3]

Purpose is the all-spice for your life. Identifying and crafting purpose is a powerful way to get clarity and make choices aligned with your highest self, the one beyond pattern, as you journey to making meaty dreams into a saucy dish you can savor now.

Purpose is a big ask (a.k.a. WTF am I doing here?). I was introduced to *life purpose* development during coaching certification. I knew the concept, but it felt big, unwieldy, and existential; plus, I had to figure out what to make for dinner—again. I didn't see people around me questioning or defining their purpose.

At the agency, we were trying to sell more shit, hoping our ideas would be chosen, and making meaning out of award shows, dancing under the light of industry luster. Purpose in advertising meant doing more than stuffing shareholders' pockets but solving a problem for society that goes beyond profit, using brand and commercial power to make a difference in the world. Often, purpose got regulated to a department, with an arresting, thought-provoking ad, designed to "go viral," making the rounds. The audience would be awed, people would feel better because they made and watched the ad, and life continued. That's as far as purpose went. Life went on with or without the guiding light of lofty purpose. I was cynical, and judgment kept real meaning at bay.

Until 2020, when I was called to coaching and found myself baring my soul to strangers in a workshop. We dove deep into fears, desires, inner saboteurs, and cheerleaders, topics I thought were only explored in the confines of a therapist's office. Definitely not on a Zoom call with nine big-hearted, curious, and open humans showing up fully in little squares. I did the visualizations, had the talks, reflected, journaled, and waded into the deep end of my pool.

> *"Finding meaning and purpose is not a five-day spa retreat. It's a fucking hike through mud and shit with golf-ball-sized hail pelting you in the face. And you have to love it. You really have to love it."*[4]
> —Mark Manson

Working with purpose, I landed with: *I am a catalyst for change using creativity and connection to build a better world.* I wasn't thrilled with the statement but felt the sentiment. Somewhere within, another version was asking to be created. After a year, this came through: *Unleashing creativity to build a better world.* Now we're talking.

Do you notice the depth and breadth of it? It is not specific and detailed but big, bold, and broad enough to hold many roads and ways of expressing this purpose. This is key because we are changeable and fluid beings, yet some things remain fixed at our core. Your purpose might change form, but it won't change meaning.

I can track everything I am doing back to purpose—unleashing creativity within myself, others, and businesses. My purpose includes all the ways creativity expresses itself through me, from writing to kitchen disco dancing, from designing to presenting. I used to live my purpose accidentally or unconsciously. The act of identifying, articulating, and connecting to my purpose helped me crystalize what has deep meaning for me, invite others to join me, and **make decisions on how and what I invest my time in.**

Crafting your purpose is how you own it. I used to feel like a wannabe, quasi-creative, not a real artist like my dad. I didn't really allow myself to own my creativity because, *What if I fail? What if I get called out? What if I never measure up?* Being "creative" never really felt like mine. I got the colorful scraps of my father's leftovers. As a kid, I got asked this question on repeat: "So, are you an artist like your father?"

I'd reply, "I write. I don't paint," which was satisfying enough to stop more questions from coming. When I crafted my purpose statement, it shifted and solidified creativity within me. Fuck yes, I am creative. Being able to own and unleash that in myself allows me to not only model it but do exactly that with others.

Coffee talk time

When it comes to the fabric of your life design, two materials are key in the stitch: purpose and values. They are deeply personal, and encompass, but go beyond, what you "do." They're who you are. Just becoming clear and aware of what moves you and really matters to you is part of your design work. *Why does this even matter?* Because getting clear on what a life well-lived looks like to *you* is not only rewarding but guiding. You're setting the foundation, not the detail. It's structural, the beams in your house; not the interior design, neither vintage floral wallpaper nor velvet or cotton couch fabrics. It defines the territory and gives you a huge playing field. Purpose and values create the frame, a space you sketch to operate and stretch in.

Your life reveals your values. Take a look. When a value is being stepped on, frustration or anger bubbles up. Look at an event that set you off recently—whether internally or externally. What important value is being dishonored? When a value is being honored and your life aligns with purpose, it feels deeply fulfilling and resonant. You're tapping in to a native frequency, a melody that moves you in a way that feels *most* like you.

Values are who you are—not who you'd like to be, not who you think you *should* be, but who you are in your life, right now. Values represent your unique and individual essence. They serve as a compass pointing out what it means to be true to yourself. When you honor your values on a regular and consistent basis, life is good and fulfilling. When you embody them daily in your choices, you feel aligned, fulfilled, and in flow. And when you dishonor them, you feel frustrated, angry, and blocked.

> *"People are all really looking for the answer to one question: 'What is right for me?'"*
>
> —Yossi Eilot, MCC, MCIL, CPCC (my certification coach)

When you live your life in alignment with what you value most, well, that's not only the hot fudge sundae but the cherry on top, bananas on the side, and thick chocolate sauce dripping from each ice cream mound like happy tears. Values are not one and done, nor a poster on a wall, but a map that guides decisions and sharpens focus. They're a looking glass into yourself.

Usually, you'll have a highest value, a value you must *absolutely honor*— or part of you dies. Looking at the landscape of my life, while honoring the generational inheritance that makes me who I am, my do-or-die value is *freedom*. Honoring this value and aligning it with my purpose is a transformative daily practice.

Learning that freedom can't be found outside of myself but a feeling I create within changes the game. It invites me to connect with what makes me feel free now, despite the circumstances. Often, it's as simple as slowing down, which is the pace of trust. When I am in the grip of fear, worrying about money, I rush, hurrying to get it all done to be safe and free already. This speed trap I set for myself is the opposite of freedom.

Once I become aware of the script I am reading from, I get to rewrite it, anchored in purpose and driven by values. But purpose is more than a felt statement. It's what you are doing when you are being exactly who you are. Designing days based on your purpose and values is how you creatively direct your life.

Fieldwork

Purpose Plunge

Reflection: Write about the times in your life when you've felt most alive and fulfilled. Identify common themes or activities. What were you doing during these peak moments, and why were they so meaningful?

Exploration: Carve out some time and space to journal and get under the skin of what drives you. Write freely and drop the judgment. When done, sit down with your favorite drink and playlist and highlight any recurring themes and insights.

Consider the following journaling prompts:
- If I had no limitations—time, money, resources—what would I spend my days doing?
- If I could wave a magic wand and change one thing in the world what would it be and why?
- What activities make me lose track of time?
- What legacy do I want to leave behind?
- What do I want people to say about me at my eightieth birthday party?

Brainstorming: Make a list of things you are good at and things you love to do, noting where they overlap. Color outside the lines and don't limit yourself. Include things you may have dismissed in the past or that seem unrealistic. How can your talents and passions serve others or contribute to something greater than yourself?

Value Mining

Identify core values. What is most important in your life? Beyond your basic human needs, what must you have in your life to experience fulfillment? Brainstorm as many values that pop into your head. Select five core values that are most important to you and reflect on why they resonate.

Fan girl or boy. Think of three to six people you most admire or love. Consider why they are so important to you. What values do they embody?

Your flag in the sand. What do you stand for? What are you willing to fight for? What is a moment when you made a difficult decision? What values drove that decision?

Anger as a signal. When was the last time you were really pissed off? Which value was being stepped on?

a creative life

I'm in Beijing without my underwear, charger, toothbrush, or clothes. I've been watching the gleaming steel baggage carousel for almost an hour, waiting for my thirty-pound backpack filled with clothes rolled like tortillas, new hiking boots, and labeled Ziplock bags to appear. Dread twists my insides. This isn't a good start to my four-week solo trip across China, Mongolia, and Russia. When it's irrefutably clear my backpack will not be arriving, I find Air China's office and open the door to the small room, and a man looks up from his desk, perplexed.

"Excuse me, sir? My bag hasn't arrived from Copenhagen, and I really need it. Can you please help me?"

Wearing a blank, solemn expression, he says, "Ticket, please." I hand him the boarding pass, and he starts typing on a beige computer out of the 1990s.

"Sorry, madam, the bag was not put on your connecting flight."

I start wringing my hands. "Do you know when it will arrive?"

He smooths his already tightly gelled black hair and replies, "No, just wait and see. You were flying with another carrier, so it's out of our hands. Give me your address, and when it comes, we'll ship it to you."

Panic rises up in my throat like bile. "But I need my bag. I won't be at one address for long. This is a four-week trip!"

Shuffling papers in an effort for me to leave, he says, "There's nothing I can do."

Distraught, alone, and sweaty, I leave the airport empty-handed into the bustling and glistening city of Beijing. Big skyscrapers reflect the sunlight, skin cream advertisements play on billboards, and throngs of people, some with livestock in shopping carts, walk across a huge overpass. The scent of fermented eggs, pickled garlic, gas, and cigarettes mix with the clang of construction, ringtones, and the roar of traffic. I'm awestruck standing in the midst of a whole new world. Despite not having even one extra T-shirt with me, I'm excited.

I buy underwear, a charger, and toiletries at Miniso, a brightly colored anime Muji for the younger gen, and a change of clothes at Zara. I start the trip with nothing but a small carry-on. I've never felt so free.

This trip teaches me how little I need. It reminds me that no matter what, I'll be okay, because I can creatively respond to whatever life serves and even have fun with it. It reminds me of the strength and creative power of the six-year-old in the Brooklyn schoolyard, the eight-year-old by the pool, the twenty-three-year-old who left New York City to go to Sri Lanka, and the countless ways I've moved with life and surfed its waves. I have nothing to fear; life and I have my back. As if on cue, my bag only reaches me when I return home to Copenhagen, and I don't need it anymore.

Creativity is how we respond to life's challenges

These challenges not only build resilience but give us an opportunity to flex our creative muscles, because something is at stake. When the right amount of pressure is applied, our performance and creativity are enhanced. Too much pressure, and we crumble like a cookie dipped too long in milk, and too little pressure leads to half-baked solutions.

Under certain conditions, stress catalyzes our creativity.[1] A pressing deadline can apply Shiatsu pressure that releases our creativity, because the brain's natural response to perceived threats or challenges can stimulate problem-solving and innovative thinking.[2] People respond differently to stress based on "neurobiological differences, different levels of internal and external resources... differing coping strategies, and trauma history."[3] That said, there are a number of universal conditions that elicit a stress response in almost everyone: novelty, unpredictability, and loss of control.[4]

According to Hans Selye, the prominent endocrinologist and father of stress, "It's not stress that kills us; it is our reaction to it."[5] Stress is not what happens to you but how you respond to it. Research shows if you can change your mind about stress, you can change your body's response to it.

"How you think and act can transform your experience of stress," explains Kelly McGonigal, health psychologist and lecturer at Stanford University. "When you choose to view stress as helpful, you create the biology of courage."[6]

I'd take this a step further: If you can change your mind, you can change your world. Standing in the middle of downtown Beijing without luggage suddenly felt like a gift. I could move freely and pick up what I needed as I traveled. It reminded me that of course I'll figure it out.

"Stress affects you on an inverted bell shaped curve, called the human performance curve. Let's go back to the hunter-gatherer days," says Heather Rusch, clinical neuroscientist and human resilience researcher. "Imagine coming out of your cave to a bush of berries. You're not very stressed about getting food. But if one day you come out to empty bushes, your stress levels increase because you're wondering how you're going to eat."

Heather pauses, blue eyes barreling into mine across the ether of Zoom. "This is the birth of creativity. It's how we created fire, tools, and eventually agriculture. You don't want to walk out to a buffet every day, but you want some stress that arises from not knowing how you're going to get your next meal. So, you want that little bit of stress, but not too much either, because then you become incapacitated, causing mental health symptoms such as depression and PTSD."

I've known Heather for years. We've witnessed many different versions of ourselves, while our cores stayed connected. We've moved through careers, relationships, and countries. Yet this is the first time I've seen Heather, the neuroscientist. She speaks powerfully, clearly, and definitively.

"The top of the curve is where creativity thrives. This healthy stress, called eustress, actually increases performance and creativity. It can also make people feel motivated and have a sense of purpose in life."

My creativity started to thrive on the Trans-Siberian trip. Hurtling across the Chinese border into Mongolia, I sat in the gold carriage, burgundy velvet curtains swinging, drank tea, and wrote for the first time in ages, rocking into a creative flow. It was the first time I had been on my own in a long time—not running from or to something but instead reconnecting to myself in the belly of a metal beast zipping through the brutal Siberian landscape. My default fast speed mode had blocked my creativity. In the quiet, it came back online.

Stress *and* her gut pushed my client and dear friend Justine to let go of a security blanket keeping her in the wrong place and into what was really calling her: a creative life. Justine's face appears on the screen, beautiful locks cascading beyond the edges of my laptop, her sketches hanging in the background. It's always good to see Justine. I ask her about what it took for her to jump into a new, creative life.

"I always had a very strong desire to be free. The traditional path never resonated with me. I went down it because I didn't know how to get to where I wanted to be without it. I had a job that was grinding down every ounce of my being. And I was like, 'Wow, I'm in the wrong place. It's really time to get out.' But there was a lot of fear, because it's not the same as quitting a job to take time off to find another job. I knew within my heart and soul this was it."

She pauses and pets her white and gray Birman cat, Lily, who rings as she walks in front of the screen, tail swishing. "I remember thinking, *I have no idea how I'm gonna get to the life that I desire. But I'm leaving this one, even though I haven't figured out the next chapter yet.* But to do that, I needed to let go of a security blanket, even though it's not that secure. We all know jobs can change; they can let you go. But the concept of having a paycheck coming in every month felt safe. Making the mental shift to *I'm never going into a job again with a plan of growing there* was really terrifying."

Justine fiddles with a sharpened pencil in her hand. It's free of chew marks, which is a big change from our initial meetings. "You remember, I was literally shaking. I had anxiety every morning. It was the most terrifying experience of my life. It's crazy to think about that now. It's been a year and a half out, and I'm more than fine. I didn't die. I still haven't entirely figured it out, but I'm a lot closer now. I have a lot more confidence. I know I will figure it out."

"What role did creativity play in this?"

Justine smiles and replies, "Creativity is the path to self-discovery. I feel at my core, at my root, like myself, even though it's still unfolding, because I'm allowing myself to be creative, try things, get curious, and throw mud at the wall. I think creativity is what all people who are lost are searching for. I know everyone's different, but it feels fundamental. Like every human should have this level of freedom to just make stuff. It makes you feel so alive."

Witnessing Justine realize she had placed herself in a cage, eyes widening, and how that self-insight opened the door made my heart swell. What followed after she hit the skies—her sketches, articles, videos, and art, and how that inspires so many—makes my heart burst.

Reclaiming your creativity is an elegant act of defiance and agency. There is so much beyond our control—actually, *everything*, except *one* thing: how we choose to respond to life. That's it, and that's enough. That choice has the power to change everything. And you, dear reader, are powerful beyond your wildest imaginings. You hold remnants of the Big Bang. Elements like carbon, oxygen, and nitrogen that make up your body were forged in the interiors of stars or in supernova explosions.

The discovery of cosmic microwave background radiation (CMB) confirmed the Big Bang theory and that the universe had always been expanding.[7] According to the Center of Astrophysics, "The cosmic microwave background is a snapshot of the oldest light in our universe, from when the cosmos was just 380,000 years old."[8] The material in our bodies has been around since the earliest moments of the universe, and we are constantly bathed in the light of the Big Bang thanks to cosmic microwave background radiation. Now, try telling me you are *not* a naturally creative and expansive being.

We are the universe expressing itself, born to create and expand. But expansion doesn't mean there is anything "wrong" with who you are now; that you need to be your *best self*, work harder, do more. That's just the same "not enough" story applied to a new "self-help" scenario. The paradox is that you are enough exactly as you are, yet you are born to expand, create, grow, and knock your potential out of the park. You can hold both: appreciation for all that you are and all that you have in *this* moment and that desire to grow and create what's next. It's a spiral, a fluid and flexible double helix, not a ladder that leads you to one destination.

The pinnacle of my creativity wasn't found in my award-winning campaign, a peanut butter rice noodle dish, or a poem but in realizing I'd been reading from someone else's script—and that I could rewrite it. I could drop the old narrative (a potent blend of societal and generational stories and childhood coping strategies) and creatively direct my life and experience. I write this as if I have figured it out—far from it. I'm finding my way into the questions more than seeking the hard and fast answers. There is really only one destination, and I'd rather be as late as possible to that grand finale party (because I really do love life, always have, even when it is hard as nails).

Deep talk, no floaties

There is nothing more creative than designing your life. It's a wildly creative act because it will lead to a new experience of it. If you keep doing the same things in the same way fueled by the same beliefs, you will recreate the same experiences with different backdrops. It would have kept Justine in a soul-grinding job, the promise of another way of living on the other side of the precipice. It would keep me picking up a ripe avocado and not eating it, believing I need to defer present pleasure to avoid future pain—until I become aware of the belief and its origins and choose to write and practice living a different one.

What you do with your pain is an art form. We can decide how we view stress and how we creatively respond to the challenges in life. There is immense freedom in the reframe and the ownership. You have the opportunity to craft your experience now. When I got fired, choosing to rock in steel cars across the Mongolian steppes showed me how creative and powerful I am.

This is an invitation to apply your innate creativity to your life in whatever way feels most useful, pleasurable, and delightful. Creativity is so much more than artistic talent, because it is not just something you *do*, it is who you *are*. It is who you are when you access and channel this transformative and somewhat elusive process (a part of me loves that neuroscience hasn't "cracked" creativity yet) to craft your own experience.

Creativity is not just something you do; it is who you are.

Recognizing the creative force within is seeing that what you listen to, how you dress, sprinkle salt on a dish, strut down the street, laugh, sign off on emails, craft a pitch, whisper to your love, write that business plan, reconcile that spreadsheet, craft a poem, dance in the dark; where you place your attention, what you choose to believe, the stories you tell about yourself and your life; what you dream about, how you kiss, how you move through the world—is all your creativity at play. And you get to choose, either consciously or on autopilot, how you want to craft your expression and experience.

You are, and always have been, free to choose. Did you forget the door was always open? Did you forget your brain has as many neurons as there are stars in the Milky Way?[9] Stale beliefs, busyness, or forgetfulness blocks your creative force and fogs up your front mirror. When that happens, pull over. Lean against the car, sip peach iced tea, and notice the moon in the cloud swept sky. Feel into the direction you're being pulled in and follow it, all while singing to your road trip playlist. You might even forget there's a destination, because the ride is so damn sweet, so you're okay with strange right turns. This *not knowing*, yet being guided and cocreating along the way, is the adventure of your lifetime.

Fieldwork

How might you nourish your creativity daily? The simplest way is to meet yourself throughout the day. Explore daily practices such as meditation, journaling, a walk in nature, being deeply present while doing the dishes, doodling, or getting lost in a good book—whatever grounds you. Set the intention of meeting yourself and the present moment as you are, as it is.

Friction point: What's the biggest challenge you're currently facing? What might be a creative way of responding to it? My dear friend Paul calls big challenges FGOs (fucking growth opportunities). How might what you're facing be a FGO?

Imagine: Choose exactly what you want to do next. What will you do? Don't overthink it; just allow the thoughts to flow and go with it. What came up for you? Will you do it? What if you spent a day choosing every next moment or activity intentionally?

transformation is honey rolling off a spoon

What did I sign up for? The meditation of pain? This is the line of thought going through my mind as I sit in "strong determination," which means without physically moving for one hour in meditation at the Vipassana Center in Sweden. My left knee is on fire, and my mind is telling me I'll never walk again because I am trying to get enlightened on a ten-day silent retreat. My thighs and calves feel dense and heavy, the pain a deep, throbbing burn.

The person next to me swallows repetitively. The scent of human musk and cedar mingle like lovers at a nightclub. All the pillows in the world won't help me now. I try to focus on my breath, but panicky thoughts flood my system. *For real, what if you pull a muscle or seriously hurt yourself? For what? You trying to be a meditation hero? What is this? Some kind of cult of pain?*

Finally, after what feels like hours, the bell chimes and I can move again. I do this three times throughout the day. On the third day of strong determination, I'm able to separate the suffering created by the stories my mind screams about the pain and the physical sensations in my body. It still hurts, but it is not agonizing. I am learning how to be with my pain. This is especially helpful after a series of fails. It's been six years since my divorce sent me reeling into the arms of an unhealthy rebound to soften the blow. That relationship only extended the ache and hardened the idea that I couldn't make it on my own. After being fired, I need to sit with my pain instead of running from it.

"Vipassana, which means to see things as they really are, is one of India's most ancient techniques of meditation." It was taught in India more than twenty-five hundred years ago as the art of living.[1] Satya Narayan Goenka, or just Goenka, was the foremost lay teacher of Vipassana meditation. Videos of his teachings, including what to expect during Vipassana, are shown at the end of a day that starts at 5:30 a.m. It's my daily saving grace. He's got a sense of humor, which I appreciate.

In one of his teachings, he says suffering arises when you expect reality—and the people in it—to be other than it is. This knocks the wind out of me. If I look back on my life, most of my disappointment and sadness came from *not* accepting things as they were and wishing they were different. It is only by accepting things as they are that we have a fighting chance of changing them.

Vipassana transforms me in subtle ways. It shows me I am strong enough to be with my pain and I don't have to be afraid of what is part of me. When I meditate daily, I show up for myself, just the way I am in that moment, get curious about my mind, and know it can be a liar. The mind makes a great servant and a pretty shitty, power-hungry boss. I discover my mind's future pattern, the focus on dreaming and scheming about tomorrow instead of being here now. I see my anxiety comes from being in the future, because it is unknown. When I do get worried, I drop into the present and ask myself:

Where are you?
I'm here.
How's here?
Pretty good, actually.
Great. So stay here.

It is not life that starts to change after being fired, breaking up, traveling on the Trans-Siberian, and sitting in silence for ten days; it's me. I have the courage to look at things and myself as they are and just be with them. I start looking for the right place to work against the clock of my work visa, which I am oddly at peace with. If I don't find a job within the month, maybe it's a sign that it's time for me to return to the States.

But I do find a job at a purpose-driven creative consultancy. I make a few requests: A four-day week and no management or board seat, just focusing on the work, which are all accepted. I enter into a beautiful collaboration with a female-run and -owned agency using creativity to drive positive change. I come home to a small one-bedroom that's all mine, hang with my neighbor who just happened to grow up in Hell's Kitchen, become part of a small community, and keep meditating and healing.

After a year of being on my own, I entered the world of dating apps for the first time. I feel like a cultural anthropologist discovering new lands. I'm able to observe how I fall for the idea of someone, perpetuating an old pattern of filling in the blanks with bold colors—not seeing people as they are but as I want them to be—and then getting hurt and disappointed when they don't live up to my imagined ideal. I discover parts of myself with each date I go on and the conversations I have with vastly different people. After a series of experiments gone weird, I end up seeing Kevin and Teddy, strangely both Danish men with American names.

Kevin has long dirty-blond hair and a solid body, works in construction, spent time in an ashram as a child, and is emotionally distant and mysterious. Teddy is earnest, kind, warm, emotionally available, interested and interesting, and plays zero games. On our first date, we met outside a church, Nikolai Kirke, in Copenhagen, to see a Leonard Cohen exhibit. We talk so much during the show, which includes a series of music and performance videos, we're shushed by people. After each date we go on, he asks, "Would you like to do this again?" to which I reply, "Yes."

Kevin and I don't have a first date. He talks his way into *passing by* for tea and ends up staying long past his due date. I do not waver and keep it all above the sheets, which intrigues and goads Kevin. He is the man I would usually choose. He's what I know. Kevin resembles my mother.

He is enigmatic, slippery, and noncommittal, which creates a certain dance. I move forward, he steps back. I'd end up trying to convince him of how wonderful I am so he can choose me, since I've abandoned myself in the process of proving my worth. I am actually able to *see* it. I see the stark choice in front of me: repeat the past or create a new future. I am aware. A note, dear readers: You cannot change what you're not aware of.

I choose the man who chooses me. Most importantly, I choose myself. I flip the bird to an old pattern, and the spell breaks because I see it. I found my person. I am a teenager again, but this time, I'm not blinded by my imagination. I see him as he is, and he sees me. We fall into one another, tumbling into the chaos and aliveness of being in love. We decided to move into my small apartment until we find another place together. His place sells faster than expected, in just a couple of weeks, and we're smashed together like avocado on toast.

A couple of days after he moves in, COVID-19 lockdown is issued. We watch *Tiger King* on Netflix, eat cheese plates in bed while drinking port wine, fuck until we ache, and play conversation games in front of my faux fireplace. I work in the living room; he works in the kitchen. His kids come over for an uncomfortable but important weekend sleepover in a homemade fort next to the couch. Instead of pulling each other's hair out, the close quarters strengthens our bond. Teddy proposes in the midnight of our bed. I say yes, and we book a date for city hall in September.

A few months later, my mom, who lives in San Miguel de Allende, has a bad fall, triggering a serious stroke. I get the call from her doctor and surgeon that she might not make it through the night and jump on the next flight to Mexico. Teddy, being younger than me, isn't vaccinated and is unable to join until weeks later, arriving at the hospital twenty minutes before my mother passes away. He catches me as I crumble and let out a blood-curdling sound that echoes through the hospital corridor.

It's August 2021, and we return home, exhausted, tear-streaked, and empty. We're on the couch zoning out to the lull of a show, when Teddy says, "Shit. Do you remember we're supposed to get married in a couple of weeks? Do you still want to do it? We can postpone if you want, really. I totally understand."

I reply, "What better way to honor life in the midst of grief than through love? Let's do it. I don't have it in me to think about place settings or organizing, but if we can keep it super simple, I'd love to get married as planned. If that's okay with you."

Teddy looks at me with tender blue eyes and says, "Then we'll do that. No fuss. Just tell me what you need, and we'll figure it out together."

We got married in September. In the short time we've been together, we survived a global pandemic, death, marriage, moving, and big career changes.

Over ten years have passed since I was divorced. I've been in therapy, been trained as a coach, been coached, traveled far and wide, sat with my pain, started a process of healing, celebrated life as it is, and have loved, lost, and gained. I've created inner shifts that have transformed my life.

Transformation is a subtle, slowly cooked meal, spices added, insides tenderized, until one day you've got the most savory dish you've ever tasted, because you created it and trusted the fire. The reality you experience is different, because you've changed.

Nothing changes unless you do. Your world is a projection of your perception, a knot of old stories, inherited beliefs, and worn-out patterns, until you unravel it and knit a new one that serves your highest self and makes this life a fucking jamboree. Because why not make it a raucous, confetti-aired, music-thumping, side-aching affair? Why not design the change you want in your life and make it real?

Transformation is not a one night stand, one and done, as much as we'd like it to be, but then we'd miss the chance to experience who we become along the way. We'd never marinate in our goo while in the chrysalis, and that's what gives us wings.

Transformation is a commitment and a continual process. Healing and conscious change are more beef bourguignon than In-N-Out Burger.

It's worth the wait.

spilled coffee and smashed cherries
a poem for those in boxes

I know what it's like to spill over
into places you're not supposed to go.

Coffee poured by an absent waitress
black liquid flowing into the saucer
"Sorry, honey," she says.
Bacon grease and White Diamonds hover
as she wipes the table
with chipped coral nails
breasts like Jell-O
threaten to escape her top.

I know what it's like to shave parts
off to fit into labeled boxes
inside a small storage room
that smells of frying oil and BO
cuts that form scabs
I pick until the skin
turns into maraschino cherries.

I know what it's like to leak,
drip, drip, dripping
feelings out the faucet
a busboy tries to fix,
sweat gathering at his brow,
unable to stop the flow.

I know what it's like to come apart,
glass slipping from hand to floor,
shards camouflaged by burnt fries
trying to find all the pieces
that can't be put together again.

The sloshing dishwasher
mingles with George Michael
telling me to have faith
reminding me that things can be stacked
and placed, made clean again,
especially if you're the one loading,
if you're a believer.

I know what it's like to be contained
and freed, again.

death and the milky way

I can tell your future. You're going to die. I know, it sucks, but this show is a limited series. It's like the reoccurring scene in *Russian Doll*, Nadia staring into the bathroom mirror, black mascara smudged, cigarette draped on her lip, after she dies and abruptly returns. Reality punches her in the gut: She's trapped reliving her thirty-sixth birthday in a cycle of party, death, repeat.[1]

Although our version might not be as entertaining or extreme, we all get a chance for a do-over every morning, until we don't. When we look at life through the lens of death, the fabric of our reality changes. The overdue Con Ed bill, the snarky email about a client you accidentally sent to all, the crickets chirping after you shared *that* post on social, your drunken karaoke rendition of Bonnie Tyler's "Total Eclipse of the Heart" all fade into irrelevance.

We watch morbid TV shows because vicarious experiences of death address our anxiety and keep our own mortality at a safe distance. That way, we can at least exert a degree of control over death. Our expiration becomes something to groan or laugh at rather than eliciting sheer terror. "Yet repeated contemplation about our eventual death could both lessen the anxiety about it and help keep us focused on the aspects of life that matter most."[2]

If you were given five years to live, would you keep doing what you're doing? If not, what would you change? Why wait to get hit with an air conditioner on the sweltering streets of New York City or feel a lump in your testicle to start living and creating the *thing* you really want to birth, all puffy and pregnant? I don't know about you, but I find this incredibly helpful. Death is like Cesar Millan, the Dog Whisperer, poking me on the neck to snap me out of fear and taking myself and life too seriously. Nothing provides a better perspective on what matters and what doesn't than death.

Let's zoom out together now, looking at our life from the vantage point of death, seeing that we're going to expire at some unknown point in time, gone, bye-bye, *arrivederci*, curtain falling, credits rolling, and you're out. What really matters? In the grand scheme of your imminent death, who cares about potential failure? Who cares what people think about your beautifully fragile creation—you know, the one asking, demanding, and pleading to be born? What do you have to lose when you will inevitably lose it all? Especially if you're creating to make a positive impact in the life of just one person. Who are you *not* to make and share it?

Steve Jobs reminded himself of his death daily. "Remembering that you are going to die is the best way I know to avoid the trap of thinking you have something to lose."[3]

I am not trying to be morbid for the sake of it but simply drawing attention to a major life event we'd all rather shove under the rug, pretending it is a long way off or that we'll bypass it altogether as though we're on the board of Google's Calico. Let the fact that you're going to expire like milk give you a kick in the peach to not only create but share that creation with the world. There's nothing like death—except for the universe, which we'll get to in a moment—to shift your perspective and activate your courage.

Another way of looking at it is from your deathbed. What will you regret *not* doing? One of the most common regrets of the dying, as told by a palliative care nurse, is: "I wish I had let myself be happier."[4] If we don't feel real happiness, we won't feel the pain of its absence. We'd rather feel the certainty of unhappiness than the uncertainty of happiness. What a rip-off. If we don't open to joy, we remain closed to life. I'd bet taking more risks to create something that really matters to you, as well as spending more time with loved ones, would make the regret list. I doubt working longer hours would feature. "I wish I stayed at the office and skipped the week in Maui," said no one ever.

Some of us get the death warning, but for many of us, my mother included, it comes swiftly and quickly and spares you little time to suddenly catch up on big dreams and quality time. When you look death in the face, whether your own or someone else's, shit gets real. It gave me a jolt to start doing the things I hesitated to do out of fear, and I am still learning how to lean into risk and more joy. I was scared of failing and falling into a financial abyss and my creative work being rejected if and when I put it out there. Now, it's not *if*, but *when*, and here we are, dear reader.

It means going all in and recapturing that youthful fearlessness, when life felt like it would never end. Now, fearlessness is driven by the knowledge that it *will* end sooner than I'd like, since I'm on the other side of forty. Research shows people who brush shoulders with death tend to seek meaning in life. If experiencing near-death situations "helps people worry less about it and devote more energy to the things that give deeper meaning to life, then focused thinking about death might help the rest of us."[5]

If you're feeling fear, the good tingling nervous excited kind, you're moving in the direction of something that really matters, unless you're on the subway heading to the Bronx past midnight, then get off the train and follow your common sense. You know what's more frightening than death? Not having really lived when you had the chance. But first, you need to figure out what *really* living means to you.

If that feels like an impossible question to answer, I got an easier one for you, like an *amuse-bouche* before the entrée arrives. What does *not* living fully look like to you? Since you can't answer me here, I'll give you mine. It's being stuck on a path set by others. It's remaining closed instead of opening. It's not risking so I'll never fail. It's not loving so I'll never lose. It's not putting myself out there so I'll never be rejected. It's giving up before I've even tried. It's not traveling to the desert to be romanced by the stars.

I'm somewhere in the Bikaner desert, in Northern India. It took a day by camel to get here, which is more like the middle of nowhere, no place. I'm a city girl, and I'm secretly proud of myself for riding the nonplussed, high-school-gum-chewing-vibes camel through the pounding heat. Every time a fly irritates my camel, which is often, she swats it with her back leg, sending me careening to the side and holding on for dear life.

I'm wrapped head-to-toe in fabric, readjusting my head scarf every hour as it eventually slides, giving the relentless sun access to my tender skin, until we arrive at a spot between dunes. We set up camp, which is basically unfolding big blankets onto the sand. The guides make a fire to cook a simple but delicious rice and dahl meal. With not much to do, we each find our own blanket, lie down, and watch the stars dart through the sky like arrows released by the universe.

It's surreal, better than the American Museum of Natural History's show at the planetarium in New York City, and Harrison Ford narrated that. Since we're in the middle of the desert, far away from the lights of any city, it's like sitting on the edge of the Milky Way, toes zigzagging in the sand. I've never seen anything as breathtakingly beautiful, never witnessed so many shooting stars piercing through the midnight velvet sky, never been so powerfully reminded that I'm on a planet spinning at one thousand miles per hour across one of two hundred billion galaxies.[6]

Later that night, under the light of the moon, we hear coyotes fighting, and it sounds vicious. The only animals I am used to are well-coiffed dogs and my Persian Creamsicle cat, Pookey, yet I'm not frightened. There's something about being under the smattering of thousands of bright stars that makes me feel safe and high on awe and wonder. I've met George Clooney, P. Diddy, Metallica, and many other "celebs" working in bars in New York, but never felt starstruck until now.

"The nitrogen in our DNA, the calcium in our teeth, the iron in our blood, the carbon in our apple pies were made in the interiors of collapsing stars. We are made of star stuff."[7]

—Carl Sagan

You can say me and those stars, we're very distant cousins.

Stars died for us to be born. When the first stars existed, the universe still didn't have enough heavy elements, like nitrogen, oxygen, and carbon, needed to form our bodies. But this changed as the first generation of stars began to die. "The majority of the atoms in my body are actually created deep inside stars in these incredibly hot stellar furnaces," says astrophysicist Suzanna Randall.[8]

You don't have to go to Northern India to be reminded of your stellar history. You can simply get into a staring contest with the moon, wake up early to see a sunrise, flirt with the stars, or look up. What really matters from this angle? What if this book tanks or my business fails? I might as well go for what I desire with abandon, joy, and some elbow grease. I'm a spiritual being having a human experience on a spinning rock in the Milky Way with no idea how I got here or where I am going after the curtain falls. The universe certainly has a dark sense of humor.

Over nineteen years, Sarah Brabant surveyed nearly one thousand students in her sociology of death and dying course at the University of Louisiana, asking how they felt about their own mortality. "The two most common responses were 'fearful' and 'pleasure in being alive,' each at 29 percent."[9] No matter how many episodes of *Russian Doll* we watch, we cannot escape awareness of our mortality. This awareness can rattle and awaken our fear or appreciation. Luckily, the choice is ours.

Let's get real

From the lens of death and the Milky Way, why *not* take the risk? Find out what you really want to do with this one precious life you've been given. But this is only the beginning. Everything doesn't magically come together when you launch that business or creative venture, write that book, or make that big change. Creating it is just the start. Now you have to inhabit the new space you've designed. This is where it gets sticky, because you've never *really* lived in this place before.

You created the blueprint, imagined its contours, but you're not used to its size. It's like moving from a one-bedroom walk-up in Queens to a palazzo in Venice. You're not used to all this space, so you set up shop in the walk-in closet instead of setting your martini down on the dusty rose marble kitchen counter and gazing out to the palm trees by the glistening pool.

Designing the life you want to inhabit and building a creative venture aligned with that juicy vision is part one. Learning how to inhabit it, well, that's part two. This is where you come face-to-face with old parts of you that kick back against the grandeur you created. The fearful, protective, inner worrier warns you not to get too comfortable, because what you created could be taken away from you. "Don't take risks. You might fail or be disappointed. Head back to 'safety,' because you don't know how it will all turn out."

The fear of all the damn newness and heightened uncertainty keep you in the closet, feeling the ends of shirts brush against you. It's natural to be scared and anxious. It's new and uncertain instead of *known* and uncertain; the fact that it's "known" makes it *feel* certain, but nothing is in this life. No certain or fixed place exists.

Enter death and the Milky Way stage left. It's natural to want certainty on this strange rock hurtling across an expanding universe, but you can create that *within*. You can be certain you got this, that no matter what is thrown your way, you'll catch it triumphantly and grow from it. Know that you're not alone in it. The universe has your back, but most importantly, you do.

You learn to inhabit this new space slowly and softly. But, you may ask, how do I invite new parts of me to take up space? How do I let old parts of me that just don't match the decor go? You become aware of what's happening within you; you can't shift what you're not aware of. You acknowledge all that fearful noise is a death rattle. The part of you keeping you small knows it's going to die because you're expanding, and it's time to let what's holding you back go. Get a self-administered shot of courage by remembering life is temporary, and the Big and Little Dippers are cheering you on.

Give your nervous system time to get used to this new level. Become aware of what you're feeling and where you are. Give yourself grace as you grow into the new space and explore new floors. Maybe you visit a room every day and spend more time in each one, running your fingers over velvety curtains, playing a tune on crystal glasses, and then going back to the smaller one where you set up camp. Until slowly, you've stopped visiting the other rooms and started living in them.

So once you've designed the outline of that gorgeous life, really step into it. Inhabit it with who you're becoming, not who you were; although thank her profusely, because she brought you here. Know it will be unknown. *That's certain.* And that's also the adventure. **Whatever you do, don't die with your magic inside you.** Someone out there needs exactly what only you can create.

Fieldwork

If you were told you had one year, six months, one month one day to live, would you do anything differently? If no, the applause sign is flashing—seriously—but if yes...

- What would you do with that time?
- Who would you spend it with?
- What would you stop doing?
- What would you keep doing?

What does being fully alive mean to you?

For me, it means:
- Loving wildly and deeply.
- Creating and connecting.
- Designing my days.
- Being of service.
- Doing things that scare me.
- Really being here, in the now.
- A slower, softer, more connected life.
- New first times.

If your time was up now, what would you regret?

Death as value alignment. Being reminded the show won't go on forever helps us live in alignment with what matters most.

- What are your five core values?
- How are they reflected in your calendar?
- How much time do you spend on what really matters to you?

momma

A poem for the survivors

She's in the way...

I make oatmeal every morning
I pick the skin on my thumb
I sing Nina Simone
I crush garlic with a wooden spoon
I trace fingers along my lover's lip
I howl between subway cars
Je danse, danse, danse
I run with mustangs, wild and free
I get a dopamine hit from a discount
I float on the surface
                    staring at a meringue moon

the end and the beginning

I've been nudged, and then shoved, into living creatively through big and small wake-up calls. *Pia to aisle seven.* Moments and events that shake me by the shoulders, flashing a light so bright, I cover my eyes. It casts shadows and reveals details that shift the way I see, well, everything. Sometimes, this feels like the end, but it's really the beginning.

Life is an album of composed moments. The light that pours through clouds, the wind rustling leaves in trees, the warm breath of my love sleeping close to me, late night laughter with friends in Paris, escargots shimmering in garlic butter, the glass my mother breaks at Viernes Sociales (Social Fridays), Cesária Évora singing in the background, and hearing her say "It's not a party unless someone breaks a glass."

The small moments stay with me. The way my mom lightly brushed and tickled my lips with her garlicky fingers when I was a kid and told me people kissed because the lips are the most sensitive part of the body. The look in her eyes when she teased people or was about to do something mischievous. The way her loud, take-over-the-room laugh mingled with a heavy cough after a lifetime of smoking. I remember how bloated her hands looked in the hospital bed. Hands that held me when I cried, rocked me, rolled joints, sprayed Chanel N°5, made small droplet pancakes upon request and cherry clafoutis, brushed hair away from my eyes, raised and clinked glasses, held paint brushes and pens, shaped clay, shaped me.

I take a photo of her hand because I never want to forget it or lose sight of any detail, the ridges on one nail, the crescent moons. But I don't need the image to remember. I've known her hands since the day I came into this world. Her right hand with its two mustard yellow fingers, the rose gold wedding band she wore until her last day, even though she got divorced decades ago. Hands that would never again move wildly in the air while telling a story, wipe dirt from my cheek with her saliva despite my protests, or draw a crown over her name when she won at Rummy 500.

In the one brief moment when my mother is lucid in the ICU, I ask her what she wants, and she looks at me with glassy green eyes I always coveted instead of my shit brown ones, and says, "I don't want to lose you."

I look right into her, her body held hostage by a stroke that paralyzes her, and say, "You'll never lose me."

I choke on emotion, the floor falls from underneath me, my knees turn to jelly, and a sadness I've never known before takes my breath away. I don't know how I am still standing. My tears and snot remind me of being in the sea in San Juan and getting pummeled by waves, coughing salt water and gasping for air. Hot tears run down my face, trying to escape the reality of this moment.

The lime green walls start to blur, and everything falls away until all that is left is love. The past, our history, the resentment for what was and what could have been—all of it evaporates, disappears, leaving love in its purest form to fill every crevice of the room. Love closes in on us, time stands still, and my heart breaks and cracks wide open, shattering into a million jagged edges, its shards slicing me open.

With this love, I touch the very essence of life, the fabric and energy of existence. In her passing, she gives me a glimpse of what's real and a rush of courage with the realization that one day, we lose everything; that this life is finite, fragile, beautiful, terrifying, and most of all, mine to live fully. Because it will end. I've got nothing to lose because I will take nothing with me.

That night, as I laid in my mother's bed in San Miguel de Allende, I didn't want to believe this was the end. I refused to. I stared at the ceiling, tears gathering in the corners of my eyes threatening to roll continuously like the sea. The wild barking of neighborhood dogs floated in through the open window. I was scared I wouldn't make it through this.

It is 2021, COVID-19 is rampant, and my husband can't join me until he is vaccinated, which turns out to be twenty minutes before my mother dies. Maybe, like poetry, this is how it is supposed to be, just my mom and I, like it was in the beginning, since I was three years old and we moved out of my dad's loft into a brownstone apartment in Brooklyn.

According to my mother, on the first day we moved in, I said, "Now that it's just me and you, we'll do things fifty-fifty." She was oddly proud, saying I had no idea what fifty-fifty even meant, lisping the equation, yet I demanded it. Now, at the end, standing at her deathbed, it is just her and I again. I watched her body slowly surrender, returning to the stardust and elements created in the first moments of the Big Bang. The history inside her not only stretches back in time but forward into a future among the stars. I imagine her raising a glass and inhaling a du Maurier on one of Saturn's rings, red toes wading in space, winking at me, blonde hair bright against the inky sky.

This moment passed because all things do, but grief stands still. My mother's death brings the most intense waves of pain I have ever felt. What remains is the memory of life's impermanence and fragility, and in this light, how little what used to seem like the big things—winning, acquiring, or achieving—matter; and just how precious the sunlight is when it streams through the windows, making patterns on the floor, while my mother grills octopus, drinks white wine with ice cubes because "I like it crisp and cold and it lasts longer that way," and makes bad jokes about my love life, giggling like a girl.

Seen from this vantage point, the risks I want to take on myself and my creativity, the joy I want to allow myself to experience, and leaving the nine-to-five that has kept me small seem like no big deal or risk at all. *Not* doing it all seems foolish and fear-laden. The sobering reality of my hidden expiration date makes risking, being open to life, and freely creating with it the only sane choice.

All I have been through has brought me here, to the work only I can do in the way only I can do it. I spent the first half of my life in fear, repeating patterns, bracing myself, blindly following someone else's script, and surrendering my true creative potential and power. I want to spend the second half of my life being moved by trust and leading from my wild heart, opening again and again to what's possible when I surrender to life, let go, and move with it instead of against it.

As someone who often clenched and braced for impact, I am still waking up to the idea that I can trust myself and the universe. I practice allowing myself to experience happiness now, not holding parts of myself back, fearing vulnerability will leave me exposed and unequipped to deal with the pain that might come my way.

I lean into joy. I linger longer in bed in the mornings with my husband instead of darting up, without an alarm clock, from the dented mattress like toast is burning, instead smelling the heady, musky scent of his night sweat mixed with Tom Ford's leather, saffron, and wood concoction, and spooning him a bit tighter. I let go of the destination and the idea that I'm not there yet; I'm always arriving to the present moment. I can see everything I need is in this moment, right here, while singing George Michael's "Careless Whisper" in the kitchen with Teddy and making scrambled eggs, the scent of roasting coffee enveloping us.

I sink into the feeling that I get to choose how I want to be in relationship with life and the beliefs I get to hold. I choose to believe *the universe is working for, with, and through me* (if I let go and stop trying to control what cannot be controlled) instead of *the universe is working against me*, and that changes my experience of life.

Fear has held me back, keeping me small for a promise of safety, but there is no real security nor permanence, only chaos, change, and creativity. And the *one* thing we control—how we creatively respond to life.

Knowing this, why not go for it? That's what I'm doing, some days really well, some days not so much. So far, activating and charging my Creative Club card has been the most rewarding and fulfilling experience of my lifetime. I hope it brings you the sense of freedom, possibility, agency, joy, and courage-inducing fear that it brought me. Creativity is your birthright and innate gift, and this is your *one* life to design.

It all starts with one simple question: What do you *really* want to create and make real in your world?

acknowledgments

Writing this book has taken me places I never imagined I'd go, and without the love and support of my family, friends, and editor, I wouldn't have had the courage to enter the deep. This involved getting dirt under my nails, drinking bottomless coffee, spending nights staring at the ceiling contemplating my existence, and having my bruised, wild heart burst.

Mom, a.k.a. *Rufina*, I felt you with me while writing this book, reminding me to "Go to bed, Ed" and listen to Amy Winehouse when I was pushing myself too hard. Thank you for showing me how to ride, wild and free, into a sunset of my own making and for encouraging me to live on my own terms. I hope, wherever you are, you pick up a copy. I adore you.

Dad, you've shown me that living a creative life is not only possible but imperative. Growing up in a world colored by your art has been a gift. Thank you for believing in me and my creativity. I remember how you shared my "choking on chicken" poem years ago, without disclosing who wrote it, and came back with rave reviews. We're each other's biggest fans. I love you to the moon and back again.

Teddy, my life partner, bestie, husband, legal advisor, and zealous cheerleader. Your love unfurls me like a sheet pulled out of the dryer. It fertilizes my creativity and feeds my voracious heart. I'm beyond grateful you're my partner in this life. Your bones are soaked in kindness. Thank you for being the hero in my story, for being a force in this book, ordering Thai takeout and me to rest, and holding loving space for this book to be born. *Jeg elsker dig.*

Shanna, my editor, creative sister goddess, forest witch, and interplanetary pegasus, thank you for seeing the shape and power of this book when I couldn't and for putting my nose in it. You encouraged me to reach into my depths in service of the story and reader and helped me craft what came tumbling out. I am forever grateful for your magic midwifery and the explosive force of our creative coupling.

Betsey, you showed me how daring to bet on your creativity and follow your pink punk heart can shape and rock culture. Your rebellious streak, effervescent energy, and zest for life found expression in the dresses you styled me in for years. Thank you for being part of this book and my life. xoxo

Christina, this book wouldn't exist without you, just as I wouldn't be who I am today without your guidance through my emotional, mental, and spiritual terrain. Ten years ago, I walked into your office a shipwreck, in tatters after a divorce. You offered me a lifeline, showing me how to rebuild, and you've been my anchor ever since. *Je t'adore, habibti.*

Heather, you're not only my dear friend but also a brilliant neuroscientist, and your insights helped shape this book. Thank you for championing both this project and me. Love you, Jellyfish.

Justine Jones, cocreating with you—whether as my client, friend, or interviewee—has been pure joy. Watching you fling open the cage door and soar has been an honor. Thank you for sharing your experiences and creative breakthroughs in this book.

Paul Ryan, my dear friend—I'm forever grateful to the Co-Active Training Institute for bringing us together. We've grown, dreamed, and bounced around wild ideas on Zoom every week since. Thank you for being my first early reader and big backer. Your unwavering support means the world to me, as do you.

Ilo Ajufo, my life has been brighter since the day you joined me in the bleachers, waiting for Amma's hug. Thank you for your feedback as an early reader and rah-rah support. The sweet escape from my four walls to your home in Abruzzo, with its donkey, peacocks that bellowed like cats, fields of wheat, and your healing company was a soothing balm in the midst of a frenzy. *Ti amo un casino.*

The fam—Stéphane, Vicki, Julie, Paul, Philippe, Mélissa, Tanja, and Bibi— thank you for jumping in right from the start and supporting this book during the presale. Knowing you're all behind me means everything.

The entire Manuscripts LLC team, thank you for supporting me in bringing this baby to life. A special thanks to Eric Koester for pulling me into this adventure, to George Thorne for making me laugh while pushing me out of my comfort zone, and to Kehkashan Khalid for the fine-tooth editing.

My gems, Christopher Calvert, Lara Mulady, and Jeppe Morgenthaler— beyond sharing our weekly horoscope, you're always there for the big moments, the times when friends are needed most. Thank you for making this book no exception.

Hayden Flohr, hearing the swoosh of your pom-poms kept me sweating on the court. Thank you for being in my corner as an early reader and cheerleader.

Sonia Cook-Broen, thank you for your thoughtful feedback on early drafts. I have a feeling we're just getting started.

Karim Miknas, *habibi*, thank you for your generous support and belief in me and this book. I'm excited to see the incredible music and art space you're going to create. Your vision has so much to offer the world.

Brett Bajema, thank you for being the first to support the presale of this book. You stopped the crickets chirping and made hope swell.

A huge shout-out to an incredible group of supporters, friends, creative partners, and collaborators who have made this book a reality. This group includes: Adam Eskow, Aline Boisset, Alix Rowland, Allie Stephens, Ana-Maria Ignat-Berget, Anders Johan Kavcic, Andrea Michalek, Andrew Panella, Angeliki Galvin, Ann-Sofi Hansen, Anthony Hammons, Ashley Ward, Brady Snow, Brian Maierhofer, Carl-Henrik Monrad-Aas, Carolynne Alexander, Caterina D'Amico, Catherine Connelly, Christina Lauer, Clint Murphy, Clint Nolan, Cole Blackburn, Daniel and Carolee Asia, David Ramos, David Shepherd, Dawn Goldworm, Emily Paul, Emma Pueyo, Frank Sieben, Gabriel Barsawme, George Rusch, Grattan Donnelly, Hannah Ernst, Hayley Creasey, Henriette Weber Andersen, Hicham Mabchour, Ivy Peltz, James Peters, Jarl Kjaerboell, Jeanne Collins, Jeanne Torre, Jeff Felten, Jena Carpenter, Jeremy Ginn, Jeremy Singh, Jes Broeng, Jess Bushnell, Jessica Reedy, John Bishop, John Brewer, John Lyons, Josefin Dirk Freij, Josh Walker, Justine Domuracki, Kat Nieh, Kathrin May, Katrine Kunst, Keith Berman, Konstanze Toerschen, Kristian Kruse, Lee Tucker, Liane AlGhusain, Linda Rusch, Lisa Ross, Luke Jermy, Mai Torvits, Manuel Saez, Maria Espinal, Maria Friis-Thorsen, Mark de Wolf, Martina Gobec, Melinda Cadwallader, Merryl Hoffman, Michael Gruber, Michael Thompson, Mike O'Connor, Natalie Wise-Ramirez, Natalie Storm, Nicola Cloherty, Oren Shai, Pamela Rubin, Parker Worth, Patrick Szajner, Rezarta Godo, Rick Kobayashi, Rishabh Gupta, Roz Duffy, Ryan Delaney, Sandra Septimius, Sarah Larsen, Shawn Carlin, Shawn Heshmatpour, Spiro Comitis, Stacey Kulongowski, Stephen O'Meara, Susanne Funder, Suzana Apelbaum, Taya Brown, Terry Toh, Thomas Golzen, Thomas Haynes, Thomas Strider, Tony Zhang, Victor Barnes, Victoria Morton, Yoshi House, Zach Michael, Zlatko Bijelic. I'm beyond grateful for your belief in my story and writing—it truly means the world to me.

Finally, to all the readers who took a chance on this book. I deeply appreciate every single one of you. May you write the grandest, most audacious script for your life and savor every minute of it.

notes

welcome to the creative club

1. Eranda Jayawickreme et al., "Post-Traumatic Growth as Positive Personality Change: Challenges, Opportunities, and Recommendations," *Journal of Personality* 89, no. 1 (September 2020): https://doi.org/10.1111/jopy.12591.

you're a card-carrying member

1. Jeffrey Davis, "The Unromantic Truth Behind Creativity Myths," *Creativity* (blog), *Psychology Today*, August 4, 2021, https://www.psychologytoday.com/us/blog/tracking-wonder/202108/the-unromantic-truth-behind-creativity-myths.
2. American Museum of Natural History, "Study Identifies Creativity Genes that Make Humans Unique," *American Museum of Natural History's Blog* (blog), April 21, 2021, https://www.amnh.org/explore/news-blogs/research-posts/human-creativity.
3. Mathias Benedek et al., "Creativity Myths: Prevalence and Correlates of Misconceptions on Creativity," *Personality and Individual Differences* 182, (November 2021): https://doi.org/10.1016/j.paid.2021.111068.
4. Vinod Menon, "20 Years of the Default Mode Network: A Review and Synthesis," *Neuron* 111, (April 2023): https://www.med.stanford.edu/content/dam/sm/scsnl/documents/Neuron_2023_Menon_20_years.pdf.
5. Jeffrey Davis, "The Unromantic Truth Behind Creativity Myths," *Creativity* (blog), *Psychology Today*, August 4, 2021, https://www.psychologytoday.com/us/blog/tracking-wonder/202108/the-unromantic-truth-behind-creativity-myths.

blackjack and the MoMA

1. Luna Park Staff, "Coney Island Cyclone," Luna Park Coney Island, accessed September 6, 2024, https://lunaparknyc.com/rides/coney-island-cyclone/.

2. The Museum of Modern Art, "Douglas Leichter," Art and Artists, Museum of Modern Art, accessed June 25, 2024, https://www.moma.org/artists/64654.

3. Mathias Benedek et al., "Creativity Myths: Prevalence and Correlates of Misconceptions on Creativity," *Personality and Individual Differences* 182, (November 2021): https://doi.org/10.1016/j.paid.2021.111068.

4. Arne Dietrich, "The Mythconception of the Mad Genius," *Frontiers in Psychology* 5, (February 2014): 79, https://www.frontiersin.org/articles/10.3389/fpsyg.2014.00079/full.

5. Jill Suttie, "Doing Something Creative Can Boost Your Well-Being," *Greater Good Magazine*, March 21, 2017, https://greatergood.berkeley.edu/article/item/doing_something_creative_can_boost_your_well_being.

6. Ibid.

7. Jeffrey Davis, "The Unromantic Truth Behind Creativity Myths," *Creativity* (blog), *Psychology Today*, August 4, 2021, https://www.psychologytoday.com/us/blog/tracking-wonder/202108/the-unromantic-truth-behind-creativity-myths.

8. Ibid.

9. Cannes Lions Staff, "Lions Content Guide 2024," Cannes Lions, accessed September 6, 2024, https://info.canneslions.com/lions-content-guide-2024/.

everything is available at the 7-Eleven within

1. Sara Rathner, "A Scarcity Mindset Can Cost You Mentally and Financially," *Credit Cards* (blog), Nerdwallet, May 31, 2023, https://www.nerdwallet.com/article/credit-cards/scarcity-money-mindset-amid-recession.

2. Aaron Benanav, "Making a Living," *The Nation*, October 2021, https://www.thenation.com/article/society/james-suzman-work/.

3. Ibid.

4. Aaron Benanav, "Making a Living," *The Nation*, October 2021, https://www.thenation.com/article/society/james-suzman-work/.

5. Raquel Reichard, "7 Age-Appropriate Ways to Talk to Kids About Money, According to Experts," *Life* (blog), Apartment Therapy, November 28, 2020, https://www.apartmenttherapy.com/how-to-teach-kids-about-money-36844033.

6. Ibid.

7. Pema Chödrön, *Start Where You Are: A Guide to Compassionate Living* (Boston, Massachusetts: Shambhala Publications, 2001).

guided by the gut

1. Alexandra Mysoor, "The Science Behind Intuition and How You Can Use It to Get Ahead at Work," *Forbes*, February 2017, https://www.forbes.com/sites/alexandramysoor/2017/02/02/the-science-behind-intuition-and-how-you-can-use-it-to-get-ahead-at-work/.

2. Tanya Carroll Richardson, "A Professional Psychic on How to Develop the 4 'Clairs' of Intuition," *MindBodyGreenMindfulness* (blog), MindBodyGreen, March 23, 2023, https://www.mindbodygreen.com/articles/the-4-types-of-intuition-and-how-to-tap-into-each.

3. Michele and Robert Root-Bernstein, "Einstein on Creative Thinking: Music and the Intuitive Art of Scientific Imagination," *Cognition* (blog), *Psychology Today,* March 31, 2010, https://www.psychologytoday.com/blog/imagine/201003/einstein-creative-thinking-music-and-the-intuitive-art-scientific-imagination.

4. Melody Wilding, "How to Stop Overthinking and Start Trusting Your Gut," *Harvard Business Review*, March 10, 2022, https://hbr.org/2022/03/how-to-stop-overthinking-and-start-trusting-your-gut.

5. Annie Jacobsen, "The US Military Believes People Have a Sixth Sense," *Time Magazine,* April 3, 2017, https://time.com/4721715/phenomena-annie-jacobsen/.

6. Shirzad Chamine, *Positive Intelligence: Why Only 20% of Teams and Individuals Achieve Their True Potential and How You Can Achieve Yours* (New York City, New York: Greenleaf Book Group Press, 2012).

7. Ibid.

8. Judit Pétervári, Magda Osman, and Joydeep Bhattacharya, "The Role of Intuition in the Generation and Evaluation Stages of Creativity," *Frontiers in Psychology* 7, (September 2016): 1420, https://doi.org/10.3389/fpsyg.2016.01420.

9. Walter Isaacson, "The Genius of Jobs" *The New York Times*, October 29, 2011, https://www.nytimes.com/2011/10/30/opinion/sunday/steve-jobs-genius.html.

10. Judit Pétervári, Magda Osman, and Joydeep Bhattacharya, "The Role of Intuition in the Generation and Evaluation Stages of Creativity," *Frontiers in Psychology 7*, (September 2016): 1420, https://doi.org/10.3389/fpsyg.2016.01420.

11. Ibid.

12. Jason Hellerman, "8 Great Frank Capra Quotes for Filmmakers," *NoFilmSchool* (blog), June 16, 2021, https://nofilmschool.com/frank-capra-quotes.

sticky scripts

1. Erika Andersen, "21 Quotes from Henry Ford on Business, Leadership and Life," *Forbes*, May 31, 2013, https://www.forbes.com/sites/erikaandersen/2013/05/31/21-quotes-from-henry-ford-on-business-leadership-and-life/.

fuck fear (do it anyway)

1. National Child Traumatic Stress Network, "Complex Trauma Effects," *What Is Child Trauma?* (blog), National Child Traumatic Stress Network, accessed June 25, 2024, https://www.nctsn.org/what-is-child-trauma/trauma-types/complex-trauma/effects.

2. Susanne Ahmari, "Neuroscience: Inside the Fear Factor," *Nature* 524, no. 34 (August 2015): 34–37, https://www.nature.com/articles/524034a.

3. Marcia Purse, "Techniques to Tame the Fight-or-Flight Response," *Living with Bipolar Disorder* (blog), *Verywell Mind,* January 12, 2024, https://www.verywellmind.com/taming-the-fight-or-flight-response-378676.

4. Julia Cameron, *The Artist's Way: A Spiritual Path to Higher Creativity* (New York City, New York: TarcherPerigee, 2002).

5. Tony Robbins, "How to Find Your Purpose," *Tony Robbins's blog* (blog), accessed June 25, 2024, https://www.tonyrobbins.com/blog/what-is-my-purpose.

6. Linda Thomas-Greenfield, "Remarks by Ambassador Linda Thomas-Greenfield at Chicago State University" (Transcript of a speech, Chicago State University, August 25, 2022).

7. Barbara Lippert, "Nike Incites Resolution," *Brand Marketing* (blog), *AdWeek*, January 7, 2008, https://www.adweek.com/brand-marketing/nike-incites-resolution-91553/.

8. Frank Ostaseski, *The Five Invitations: Discovering What Death Can Teach Us About Living Fully* (New York City, New York: Flatiron Books, 2017).

9. Beau Lotto, "The Neuroscience of Perception—An Interview with Beau Lotto, PhD," interviewed by Daniel Stickler, *Qualia's Blog* (blog), June 6, 2022, https://qualialife.com/the-neuroscience-of-perception-an-interview-with-beau-lotto-ph-d/.

10. Mark Divine, "The Breathing Technique a Navy SEAL Uses to Stay Calm and Focused," *Time Magazine*, May 4, 2016, https://time.com/4316151/breathing-technique-navy-seal-calm-focused/.

la dolce far niente is doing something

1. Very Big Brain, "Tapping into the Default Mode Network (DMN): Unlocking Creativity and Mind-Wandering," *Brain Anatomy* (blog), *Very Big Brain*, March 11, 2023, https://verybigbrain.com/brain-anatomy/tapping-into-the-default-mode-network-dmn-unlocking-creativity-and-mind-wandering/.

2. Jay Dixit, "We're Doing Downtime Wrong," *Cognitive Capacity Productivity* (blog), NeuroLeadership Institute, November 19, 2021, https://neuroleadership.fi/blog/were-doing-downtime-wrong/.

3. Stacey Colino, "The Science of Why You Have Great Ideas in the Shower," *National Geographic*, August 2022, https://www.nationalgeographic.com/magazine/article/the-science-of-why-you-have-great-ideas-in-the-shower.

4. Ted Bauer, "Insights: What Are They, Why Do They Matter, and How Do You Generate More of Them?" *Culture and Leadership* (blog),

NeuroLeadership Institute, September 2, 2021, https://neuroleadership.fi/blog/insights-what-are-they-why-do-they-matter-and-how-do-you-generate-more-of-them/.

5. David Rock, Daniel J. Siegel, Steven A.Y. Poelmans, and Jessica Payne, "The Healthy Mind Platter," *NeuroLeadership Journal*, no. 4 (October 2012), https://davidrock.net/files/02_The_Healthy_Mind_Platter_US.pdf.

6. Stacey Colino, "The Science of Why You Have Great Ideas in the Shower," *National Geographic*, August 2022, https://www.nationalgeographic.com/magazine/article/the-science-of-why-you-have-great-ideas-in-the-shower.

7. Joseph Carroll, "Imagination, the Brain's Default Mode Network, and Imaginative Verbal Artifacts," in *Evolutionary Perspectives on Imaginative Culture*, eds. Joseph Carroll, Mathias Clasen, and Emelie Jonsson (Cham, CH: Springer, 2020), 25–45, https://doi.org/10.1007/978-3-030-46190-4_2.

8. Nancy C. Andreasen, "Secrets of the Creative Brain," *The Atlantic,* July/August 2014, https://www.theatlantic.com/magazine/archive/2014/07/secrets-of-the-creative-brain/372299/.

9. Graham Wallas, *The Art of Thought* (New York City, New York: Harcourt, Brace and Company, 1926).

10. Stacey Colino, "The Science of Why You Have Great Ideas in the Shower," *National Geographic*, August 2022, https://www.nationalgeographic.com/magazine/article/the-science-of-why-you-have-great-ideas-in-the-shower.

11. Ibid.

now is later (eat the avocado)

1. Gina Ryder, "What Is Neuroplasticity?" *Health* (blog), *Psych Central*, November 12, 2021, https://psychcentral.com/health/what-is-neuroplasticity#how-it-works.

2. Vida Demarin, Sandra Morovic, and Raphael Béné, "Neuroplasticity," *Periodicum Biologorum* 116, no. 3 (September 2014): 209–11. https://www.researchgate.net/publication/289103406_Neuroplasticity.

3. Susan Rieck, "The Brain and Our Habits: Natural Pathways to Wellness," *Our Insights* (blog), Maximus, August 25, 2021, https://maximus.com/the-brain-our-habits.

4. Eagle Gamma, "Brain Plasticity (Neuroplasticity): How Experience Changes The Brain," *Biopsychology* (blog), *Simply Psychology*, August 17, 2023, https://www.simplypsychology.org/brain-plasticity.html.

champagne problems

1. Rachel Hall, "Drugs and Alcohol Do Not Make You More Creative, Research Finds," *The Guardian*, March 24, 2023, https://www.theguardian.com/science/2023/mar/24/drugs-and-alcohol-do-not-make-you-more-creative-research-finds.
2. Elle Hunt, "'I Thought Drink and Drugs Enabled My Creativity': Julia Cameron on the Drama Behind *The Artist's Way*," *The Guardian*, August 18, 2022, https://www.theguardian.com/books/2022/aug/18/i-thought-drink-and-drugs-enabled-my-creativity-julia-cameron-on-the-drama-behind-the-artists-way.
3. John von Radowitz, "Drunk Writers Were Better Sober, Says Psychiatrist," *The Independent*, June 25, 2010, https://www.independent.co.uk/news/science/drunk-writers-were-better-sober-says-psychiatrist-2010053.html.
4. Laurie Martin, "Alcohol and Drugs Boost Creativity? Think Again," *Psychiatric Times Blog* (blog), June 29, 2010, https://www.psychiatrictimes.com/view/alcohol-and-drugs-boost-creativity-think-again.
5. John von Radowitz, "Drunk Writers Were Better Sober, Says Psychiatrist," *The Independent*, June 25, 2010, https://www.independent.co.uk/news/science/drunk-writers-were-better-sober-says-psychiatrist-2010053.html.
6. Mirror.co.uk, "Amy Winehouse: Is Art Worth Dying For?" *The Mirror*, July 25, 2011, https://www.mirror.co.uk/3am/celebrity-news/amy-winehouse-is-art-worth-dying-143804.
7. Nancy C. Andreasen, "Secrets of the Creative Brain," *The Atlantic*, July/August 2014, https://www.theatlantic.com/magazine/archive/2014/07/secrets-of-the-creative-brain/372299/.
8. University of Essex, "Sparking Creativity: Meditation and Training Are Better than Drugs and Alcohol," *Science News* (blog), *SciTechDaily*, March 28, 2023, https://scitechdaily.com/sparking-creativity-meditation-and-training-are-better-than-drugs-and-alcohol/.

9. Terry Gross, "David Sedaris on the Life-Altering and Mundane Pages of His Old Diaries," *Fresh Air Author Interviews* (blog), NPR, May 31, 2017, https://www.npr.org/2017/05/31/530810011/david-sedaris-on-the-life-altering-and-mundane-pages-of-his-old-diaries.

you're the secret sauce

1. Elizabeth Gilbert, "'Be Yourself. Everyone Else Is Taken.' Oscar Wilde Good Morning, Beautifuls" *Elizabeth Gilbert's Blog* (blog), July 26, 2013, https://www.elizabethgilbert.com/be-yourself-everyone-else-is-taken-oscar-wilde-good-morning-beautifuls/.
2. Jussi Valtonen, "The Health Benefits of Autobiographical Writing: An Interdisciplinary Perspective," *Journal of Medical Humanities* 42, no. 4 (December 2021): 1–19, https://www.ncbi.nlm.nih.gov/pmc/articles/PMC8664792/.
3. Zorana Ivcevic Pringle, "Where Creative Potential Comes From," *Creativity* (blog), *Psychology Today,* September 22, 2020, https://www.psychologytoday.com/us/blog/creativity-the-art-and-science/202009/where-creative-potential-comes.
4. Jussi Valtonen, "The Health Benefits of Autobiographical Writing: An Interdisciplinary Perspective," *Journal of Medical Humanities* 42, no. 4 (December 2021): 1–19, https://www.ncbi.nlm.nih.gov/pmc/articles/PMC8664792/.
5. Ibid.

hello there good-looking (meet your future self)

1. Stephen A. Fadare, Ermalyn P. Lambaco, Yasmin B. Mangorsi, Louise J. D. Lorchano, and Juvenmile B. Tercio, "A Voyage into the Visualization of Athletic Performances: A Review," *American Journal of Multidisciplinary Research and Innovation* 1, no. 3 (August 2022): 105–109, https://doi.org/10.54536/ajmri.v1i3.479.

2. Lidija Globokar, "The Power of Visualization and How to Use It," *Forbes*, March 5, 2020, https://www.forbes.com/sites/lidijaglobokar/2020/03/05/the-power-of-visualization-and-how-to-use-it.

3. Stephen A. Fadare, Ermalyn P. Lambaco, Yasmin B. Mangorsi, Louise J.D. Lorchano, and Juvenmile B. Tercio, "A Voyage into the Visualization of Athletic Performances: A Review," *American Journal of Multidisciplinary Research and Innovation* 1, no. 3 (August 2022): 105–109, https://doi.org/10.54536/ajmri.v1i3.479.

4. Swapnil Dhruv Bose, "When Jim Carrey Wrote Himself a $10 Million Cheque," *Far Out Magazine*, September 8, 2022, https://faroutmagazine.co.uk/jim-carrey-wrote-himself-10-million-cheque/.

5. Stephen A. Fadare, Ermalyn P. Lambaco, Yasmin B. Mangorsi, Louise J.D. Lorchano, and Juvenmile B. Tercio, "A Voyage into the Visualization of Athletic Performances: A Review," *American Journal of Multidisciplinary Research and Innovation* 1, no. 3 (August 2022): 105–109, https://doi.org/10.54536/ajmri.v1i3.479.

6. Nona Djavid, "Two Missing Pieces of the Be, Do, Have Model," *Forbes,* September 25, 2023, https://www.forbes.com/sites/forbesbusinesscouncil/2023/09/25/two-missing-pieces-of-the-be-do-have-model/.

we run in creative packs

1. Cody Delistraty, "The Myth of the Lone Creative Genius," *At Large* (blog), *Document Journal*, January 20, 2022, https://www.documentjournal.com/2022/01/the-myth-of-the-lone-creative-genius/.

2. Joshua Wolf Shenk, "The End of 'Genius,'" *The New York Times*, July 19, 2014, https://www.nytimes.com/2014/07/20/opinion/sunday/the-end-of-genius.html.

3. Elizabeth Gilbert, "Your Elusive Creative Genius," February 2009, video and transcript, 00:19:14, https://www.ted.com/talks/elizabeth_gilbert_your_elusive_creative_genius/transcript.

4. Cody Delistraty, "The Myth of the Lone Creative Genius," *At Large* (blog), *Document Journal*, January 20, 2022, https://www.documentjournal.com/2022/01/the-myth-of-the-lone-creative-genius/.

5. The Nobel Prize, "The Myth of the Lone Genius," *Nobel Prize Outreach* (blog), Nobel Prize, accessed July 17, 2024, https://www.nobelprize.org/martin-chalfie-npii-canada/.

6. Fernando Teixeira and Izabela Cardozo, "The 'Lone Genius' Myth: Why Even Great Minds Collaborate," BBC, March 12, 2021, https://www.bbc.com/worklife/article/20210308-the-lone-genius-myth-why-even-great-minds-collaborate.

7. Cody Delistraty, "The Myth of the Lone Creative Genius," *At Large* (blog), *Document Journal*, January 20, 2022, https://www.documentjournal.com/2022/01/the-myth-of-the-lone-creative-genius/.

8. Fernando Teixeira and Izabela Cardozo, "The 'Lone Genius' Myth: Why Even Great Minds Collaborate," BBC, March 12, 2021, https://www.bbc.com/worklife/article/20210308-the-lone-genius-myth-why-even-great-minds-collaborate.

9. Megan Hennessey, "Architecture Professor Debunks 'Lone Genius' Myth in New Book," *News* (blog), Northeastern University College of Arts, Media and Design, November 28, 2023, https://camd.northeastern.edu/news/architecture-professor-debunks-lone-genius-myth-in-new-book/.

10. Joshua Wolf Shenk, "The End of 'Genius,'" *The New York Times*, July 19, 2014, https://www.nytimes.com/2014/07/20/opinion/sunday/the-end-of-genius.html.

11. Encyclopaedia Britannica, 15th ed. (Chicago, IL: Encyclopaedia Britannica, 2024), s.v. "Muse." https://www.britannica.com/topic/Muse-Greek-mythology.

12. Elaine Sciolino, "Can Robots Replace Michelangelo?" *Smithsonian Magazine,* December 2023, https://www.smithsonianmag.com/innovation/can-robots-replace-michelangelo-180983240/.

13. Paul Brian, "The Key Problem with the Myth of the Lone Genius," *Ideapod* (blog), November 15, 2022, https://ideapod.com/the-myth-of-the-lone-genius/.

velour revolutions

1. *The New York Times*, "Winners of Coty Awards," *The New York Times,* June 23, 1971, https://www.nytimes.com/1971/06/23/archives/winners-of-coty-awards.html.

2. The Museum of Modern Art, "Douglas Leichter," Museum of Modern Art, accessed June 25, 2024, https://www.moma.org/artists/64654.

3. Rachel Syme, "How Betsey Johnson Built a Fashion Empire and Lost Her Name," *The New Yorker,* May 20, 2020, https://www.newyorker.com/culture/on-and-off-the-avenue/how-betsey-johnson-built-a-fashion-empire-and-lost-her-name.

4. Lillian Gissen, "Fashion Designer Betsey Johnson, 80, Reveals Shocking Reason She Got Married with NO PANTS on when She Tied the Knot with Velvet Underground Cofounder John Cale in 1968," *Daily Mail,* July 20, 2023, https://www.dailymail.co.uk/femail/article-12320541/Fashion-designer-Betsey-Johnson-80-reveals-shocking-reason-got-married-NO-PANTS-tied-knot-Velvet-Underground-founder-John-Cale-1968.html.

5. Liana Satenstein, "Long Live Betsey Johnson," *Paper Magazine,* February 2024, https://www.papermag.com/betsey-johnson#rebelltitem19.

6. Betsey Johnson Staff, "Betsy Johnson: An Icon of American Fashion," Betsey Johnson, accessed June 25, 2024, https://betseyjohnson.com/pages/betseys-bio.

7. Kristin Anderson, "That Girl: An Oral History of Betsey Johnson," *Vogue,* May 26, 2015, https://www.vogue.com/article/betsey-johnson-cfda-awards.

8. Nadezhda Tolokonnikova, *Read & Riot: A Pussy Riot Guide to Activism* (New York City, New York: HarperCollins, 2018), "Rule No. 9: Create Alternatives," https://theanarchistlibrary.org/library/nadezhda-tolokonnikova-read-riot.

9. Nancy C. Andreasen, "Secrets of the Creative Brain," *The Atlantic,* July/August 2014, https://www.theatlantic.com/magazine/archive/2014/07/secrets-of-the-creative-brain/372299/.

10. Nadezhda Tolokonnikova, *Read & Riot: A Pussy Riot Guide to Activism* (New York City, New York: HarperCollins, 2018), "Rule No. 2: Do It Yourself," https://theanarchistlibrary.org/library/nadezhda-tolokonnikova-read-riot.

11. Alfred Balkin, "What Is Creativity? What Is It Not?" *Music Educators Journal* 76, no. 9 (May 1990): 29–32, https://doi.org/10.2307/3401074.

12. Steven Kotler, "Einstein at the Beach: The Hidden Relationship Between Risk and Creativity," *Forbes*, October 2012, https://www.forbes.com/sites/stevenkotler/2012/10/11/einstein-at-the-beach-the-hidden-relationship-between-risk-and-creativity.

13. Jackie Huba, "What Lady Gaga Can Teach You About Being the Best at Work," *CNN Business* (blog), CNN, May 28, 2013, https://edition.cnn.com/2013/05/26/business/lady-gaga-business-route-to-the-top/index.html.

14. Steven Kotler, "Einstein at the Beach: The Hidden Relationship Between Risk and Creativity," *Forbes*, October 2012, https://www.forbes.com/sites/stevenkotler/2012/10/11/einstein-at-the-beach-the-hidden-relationship-between-risk-and-creativity.

your life manual

1. Matt Seybold, "The Apocryphal Twain: 'The Two Most Important Days of Your Life...'" *The Apocryphal Twain* (blog), Center for Mark Twain Studies, December 6, 2016, https://marktwainstudies.com/the-apocryphal-twain-the-two-most-important-days-of-your-life/.

2. Mara Gordon, "What's Your Purpose? Finding a Sense of Meaning in Life is Linked to Health," *Your Health* (blog), NPR, May 25, 2019, https://www.npr.org/sections/health-shots/2019/05/25/726695968/whats-your-purpose-finding-a-sense-of-meaning-in-life-is-linked-to-health.

3. John Templeton Foundation Staff, "Purpose," John Templeton Foundation, accessed June 25, 2024, https://www.templeton.org/discoveries/the-psychology-of-purpose.

4. Mark Manson, "Find What You Love and Let It Kill You," *Mark Manson* (blog), September 19, 2013, https://markmanson.medium.com/find-what-you-love-and-let-it-kill-you-20df975bd1c3.

a creative life

1. Jeffrey Davis, "How 'Good Stress' Helps Creativity in the Workplace," *Stress* (blog), *Psychology Today*, August 24, 2016, https://www.psychologytoday.com/intl/blog/tracking-wonder/201608/how-good-stress-helps-creativity-in-the-workplace.

2. Braden Becker, "The Surprising Relationship Between Stress and Creativity," *HubSpot's Blog* (blog), February 6, 2018, https://blog.hubspot.com/marketing/relationship-between-stress-and-creativity.

3. Danielle Render Turmaud, "Why Stress Affects People Differently," *Stress* (blog), *Psychology Today,* March 31, 2020, https://www.psychologytoday.com/us/blog/lifting-the-veil-trauma/202003/why-stress-affects-people-differently.

4. Juliana Nery Souza-Talarico et al., "Cross-Country Discrepancies on Public Understanding of Stress Concepts: Evidence for Stress-Management Psychoeducational Programs," *BMC Psychiatry* 16, no. 181 (June 2016): 1–9, https://doi.org/10.1186/s12888-016-0886-6.

5. Timothy D. Brewerton and Kathleen T. Brady, "The Role of Stress, Trauma, and PTSD in the Etiology and Treatment of Eating Disorders, Addictions, and Substance Use Disorders," in *Eating Disorders, Addictions and Substance Use Disorders*, ed. Timothy D. Brewerton and Amy Baker Dennis (Berlin, Heidelberg: Springer, 2014), 243–258. https://doi.org/10.1007/978-3-642-45378-6_17.

6. Kelly McGonigal, "How to Make Stress Your Friend," YouTube, September 4, 2013, 00:14:28, https://www.youtube.com/watch.

7. Dr. Edward J. Wollack, "Universe 101—Tests of Big Bang: The CMB," *Universe* (blog), NASA, February 20, 2024, https://map.gsfc.nasa.gov/universe/bb_tests_cmb.html.

8. Harvard & Smithsonian Center for Astrophysics Staff, "Cosmic Microwave Background," *Harvard and Smithsonian Center for Astrophysics's Blog* (blog), accessed July 8, 2024, https://www.cfa.harvard.edu/research/topic/cosmic-microwave-background.

9. Nancy C. Andreasen, "Secrets of the Creative Brain," *The Atlantic,* July/August 2014, https://www.theatlantic.com/magazine/archive/2014/07/secrets-of-the-creative-brain/372299/.

transformation is honey rolling off a spoon

1. S.N. Goenka, "Vipassana Meditation," Vipassana Meditation, Dhamma.org, accessed June 25, 2024, https://www.dhamma.org/en-US/about/vipassana.

death and the milky way

1. *Russian Doll,* "Nothing in This World Is Easy," directed by Leslye Headland (2019; Universal Television, 2019), 25 min, Video.
2. Michael W. Wiederman, "Thinking about Death Can Make Life Better," *Scientific American,* March 2015, https://www.scientificamerican.com/article/thinking-about-death-can-make-life-better/.
3. Marcel Schwantes, "Steve Jobs Said This Was the Most Important 'Tool' He Had Ever Encountered to Make the Most of His Life," *Lead* (blog), Inc., December 13, 2019, https://www.inc.com/marcel-schwantes/steve-jobs-said-this-is-most-important-tool-he-ever-encountered-to-make-most-of-his-life.html.
4. Elsa Vulliamy, "The Most Common Regrets of the Dying, According to a Palliative Care Nurse," *The Independent,* February 3, 2016, https://www.independent.co.uk/life-style/palliative-nurse-shares-the-most-common-regrets-of-her-patients-a6821061.html.
5. Michael W. Wiederman, "Thinking about Death Can Make Life Better," *Scientific American,* March 2015, https://www.scientificamerican.com/article/thinking-about-death-can-make-life-better/.
6. Alastair Gunn, "How Many Galaxies Are There in the Universe?" *BBC Sky at Night Magazine,* March 18, 2024, https://www.skyatnightmagazine.com/space-science/how-many-galaxies-in-universe/.
7. Anna Frebel, "We're More Than Stardust—We're Made of the Big Bang Itself," Accessed July 8, 2024, Big Think, New York, Transcript and Video, 00:03:15, https://bigthink.com/videos/anna-frebel-on-the-big-bang/.

8. Robert Lea, "Are We Really Made of 'Star Stuff' and What Does That Even Mean?" *The Universe* (blog), Space.com, August 21, 2023, https://space.com/we-are-made-of-star-stuff-meaning-truth.

9. Michael W. Wiederman, "Thinking about Death Can Make Life Better," *Scientific American*, March 2015, https://www.scientificamerican.com/article/thinking-about-death-can-make-life-better/.

Printed in Great Britain
by Amazon